HOW TO BE A CHRISTIAN
EVEN IF YOU ALREADY ARE ONE

WILLIAM H. SHANNON

**HOW TO BE A CHRISTIAN
EVEN IF YOU ALREADY ARE ONE**

©2012 by William H. Shannon

All rights reserved

ISBN 978-1-60458-871-2

DEDICATION

To Lisa Hartmann

Without her dedicated assistance

this book

would never have reached completion.

ACKNOWLEDGEMENTS

I want to thank the following Sisters for the invaluable help they have given in bringing this book to publication: Kathy Weider and Mary Anne Turner for the cover art, and Mary Anne for preparing the manuscript.

CONTENTS

Introduction 3

Chapter One: Learning to Read the Bible..7

Chapter Two: Thomas Merton and a New Way of Understanding
    Prayer 7

Chapter Three: My Conversion to a New Way of Understanding Peace
    and Non-Violence...107

Chapter Four: My Conversion to a New Way of Understanding
    Church..135

INTRODUCTION

HOW TO BECOME A CHRISTIAN EVEN IF YOU ARE ALREADY ONE

I recall being some years ago in Hawley Cooke Bookstore in Louisville, KY. I was browsing in the religious books section (probably looking to see whether they were carrying some of my books). A rather serious-looking young man was there also and we had a brief talk. Then suddenly he asked: "Have you been born again?" With some enthusiasm I replied: "Indeed I have been born again and again and again and again." He obviously was not prepared for my answer. He frowned a bit, and then just walked away without saying another word.

In chapter three of the Fourth gospel, Jesus tells Nicodemus that he must be born again. The Greek word used here *anothen* (ανωθεν) can also mean: be born anew. Being born again or being born anew is the on-going story of every Christian.

Indeed at the human level it is the story of every human being. A baby is born into a child, a child into an adolescent, an adolescent into an adult. We don't stop being born again and again as adults. The same principle applies to our lives as Christians. We are pilgrims on a journey and we change as we move along. That is the basic meaning of the word "conversion" (*convertere*: to turn around). We change as we travel through life. The changes are not only physical and psychological. There are also changes in the way we think about life and the values that make life worth living.

There are also changes in faith, in faith-perception. Your faith, my faith, is not the same today as it was ten years ago. Or at least it shouldn't be.

John Henry Newman,-- whose thinking of more than a century ago anticipated a new direction in the Church that came to fruition in the Second Vatican Council--, once made the following statement: "In a higher world it is otherwise; but here below, to live is to change; to be perfect is to have changed often."

For a long time I've puzzled over these words of Newman. I wondered what he meant by the word "perfect." Then the thought came to me that he may have had in mind Matthew's words in the Sermon on the Mount (Mt.5-48): "Be perfect as your heavenly father is perfect." I checked a Greek dictionary and found that the word Matthew used, namely, *teilos*, has the meaning of "complete." So it seemed to me that that may be what Newman had in mind, namely that our goal as followers of Jesus is to become "complete Christians." That is fully and totally Christian in all aspects of our lives.

True, we are Christians, yet –if we are truly alive spiritually – we keep growing into our Christian faith. My point is that there are elements of our thinking and acting that have not yet been fully Christianized. There are bits of us not yet touched by the grace of Christ and the Spirit.

That is what I mean by my title: "How to become a Christian, even if you are already one." Conversion is the personal transformation whereby we who are already

Christians are in the process of becoming more fully Christians.

In a letter to his friends in September 1968- before his departure for Asia- Thomas Merton wrote; "*Our real journey in life is interior: it is a matter of growth, deepening, and of an ever greater surrender to the creative action of love and grace in our hearts.*"

This book is about the conversions I have gone through since I became a priest in 1943. I single out four major conversion experiences- all were stepping stones toward a better awareness of what it means for me to be a Christian.

Reflecting on these conversion experiences calls to mind images from a favorite movie of mine, "The Dead Poets Society". As I remember the movie, it's about Mr. Keating, the new teacher at a fashionable boy's school. Keating saw education as a kind of conversion experience: for it was moving to a new level of understanding. One day in class Keating suddenly jumped up on top of his desk and said: "The perspective from up here is very different from the one you get sitting at your desk." Then he made them all stand on their desks to get a new perspective. On another occasion he had them tear out of their textbooks the pages that explained to them the meaning of the literature they were going to read. He wanted them to have a first-hand experience of the text. They must read through their own eyes and not through someone else's.

A true conversion changes you so much that you see life and reality in altogether different ways. But because reality is multifaceted, you need to go through more than one conversion before you can enter fully into the mystery of God who is at the heart of all reality. As we go through life and try to grasp its depths we have a number of conversion experiences.

Of the conversion experiences that I've had in my life I want to mention four major experiences that are especially important to me. I will list the four and then devote a chapter to each one.

The four conversions were:

1. a newer and better way of reading the bible that I learned from contact with the biblical movement;
2. a new understanding of prayer, contemplation and the mystical element of the church that came to me from the writings Thomas Merton;
3. a new understanding of peace making and non-violence that also came to me through the influence of Thomas Merton;
4. the wonderful experience of living through the years of the Second Vatican Council (1962-65) and being irrevocably changed in my way of thinking about the Church. I came to see that the church was not only or just the hierarchy; primarily and most importantly the church is the people of God.

CHAPTER ONE
LEARNING TO READ THE BIBLE

"Ignorance of Scripture is ignorance of Christ" – St. Jerome

My first major conversion experience was to the biblical movement. For years I had paid little attention to the bible. After all, I was a Catholic and wasn't the Bible a Protestant book? Actually I knew it wasn't, but it almost seemed as if we thought it was. We didn't so much read it as use it. Scripture was a tool that we used to prove theological positions we already believed.

What contact with the biblical movement did for me was to help me see that the Bible is God's self revelation, but that revelation carried in fragile vessels of time-conditioned documents written by authors who were products of their history and who shared the mentality of their time. This meant that historical and literary criticism, with all that this involves, is necessary before we can discover what the Bible is saying to us. First we have to know what the Scriptures were saying to their own times. Then we are in a better position to relate this meaning to our own times and circumstances.

For the first time I was really reading the Bible to hear what it said. This was a truly liberating experience for me. It opened up the whole world of the Bible for me. It was an experience of conversion to a new way of listening to God. It was a eureka experience! I was standing on my desk and I was tearing up old notes. How about you? If you are a Catholic, have you been standing on any desks lately and tearing up any old notes? My scripture professor probably would not like what I am saying; but, since he has now gone to God, he knows all this much better than I do. Actually he may be pleased that I would be learning things about the Bible that he would like to have taught but was afraid to do so. The fear of accusations of Modernism was still very threatening to him at that time in the life of the church.

What Is The Biblical Movement?

The biblical movement has to do with identifying the meaning of a document as clearly as possible. This is done by studying the text, the culture, the literary forms that are used and the author or authors of the document. I don't want to go into this in detail. I will just take the Gospels as an example of the kind of reflection that must be made on the text.

First of all I want to point out that in the New Testament the word "Gospel" always refers to the *oral* proclamation of salvation and never to something fixed in writing. The New Testament knows only the one Gospel; the Gospel of salvation in Jesus Christ. To put "Gospel" into the plural, therefore would falsify its very nature. From the second century onward however, there are references to Gospels meaning the written accounts of the one Gospel. It is important to know that the books of the New Testament, as they are arranged in the Bible, are not in chronological order. Maybe I knew this but never thought of how important this insight is. Anyway, in our bibles the four Gospels are placed at the beginning of the New Testament, followed then by the Letters of Paul and other books (Letters of John and of Peter, etc.) *Yet the Gospels were written several decades after Paul's letters.* This difference indicates the crucial importance of Paul's letters in handing on the Christian message. For instance, the earliest testimony to the resurrection of Jesus is found in Chapter 15 of *First Corinthians. This long antedates the Gospel narratives of the resurrection.*

Another aspect of the Gospels that needs to be made clear as very important is the fact that there are 3 levels of meaning in the Gospels.

Level 1: The historical level; what Jesus said and did. Because of the obvious fact that no one was around to give an account of everything that Jesus said and did this level is not recoverable.

Level 2: This level embraces the stories about Jesus words and actions that existed among the early followers of Jesus, but which were not as yet put into writing. This would be the Gospel material in the pre-literary period. Don't you wish that you could be in touch with some of these early witnesses to the words and deeds of Jesus? Actually that wish can be satisfied somewhat at least because there is a third level of meaning in the Gospels.

Level 3: This is the level of meaning that we find in our bibles. This may be called the Gospel meaning. This level would be the meaning that we find today in our bibles. Luke expresses this well in the very beginning of his Gospel where he says, "Since many have undertaken to compile a narrative of the events that have been fulfilled among us, just as those who were eye witnesses from the beginning and ministers of the word have handed them down to us, I too have decided, after investigating everything accurately anew, to write it down in an orderly sequence for you, most excellent Theophilus, so that you may realize the certainty of the teaching you have received."

For it was precisely from these oral accounts of the deeds and sayings of Jesus that the Gospel writers narrated the Jesus story. This was their insight in the light of their belief in Jesus' resurrection. Note: Luke indicates that he was not an eye- witness but consulted eye witnesses. The Pontifical Biblical Commission

J.A. Fitzmyer in his commentary on the instruction of the Biblical Commission on the 1966 document on the historical truth of the Gospel says:

> The most significant thing in the whole document, when all is said and done, is that the Biblical Commission calmly and frankly admits that what is contained in the Gospels as we have them today, is not the words and deeds of Jesus in the first stage of tradition, nor even the form in which they were preached in the second stage, but only in the form compiled and edited by the evangelists. This form, however, reflects the two previous stages and the second more than the first. It is good to recall that this redacted form of the sayings and deeds of Jesus which the evangelists give us is the inspired form. The evangelists were inspired by the Holy Spirit to compile and write down the accounts as they did.

This inspiration guarantees that the Gospel truth [namely the truth related to our salvation] is free from errors.

Father Barnabas M. Ahern

Father Barnabas M. Ahern sums up so beautifully this development of the Gospel material in this truly poetic piece:

The floor of the ocean is littered with sea shells. Only some of these are swept onto the shore. There wind and rain smooth away sharp edges. The sunlight brings out rich coloring. A man finds them there, gathers them up and forms them into a vase, beautiful in shape and color. To appreciate the exquisite beauty of the vase we not only gaze at its whole contour and color pattern, but we study also the graceful turn and delicate tint of every shell. It is the same with the Gospels.

(Level 1) Our Lord's life was like an ocean bed filled with words and deeds in such abundance that books could not contain them.

(Level 2) Only some of these reached the shore of the primitive community. There the wind and light of the Spirit shaped the telling of each deed and illumined its deep meaning.

(Level 3) The evangelists gathered together these living memories and molded them into a Gospel under the light of the Spirit. No two Gospels are the same; each has its own contour and coloring.

To measure the truth and to appreciate the beauty of the Gospels, we cannot be content to study merely the formative work of the evangelist and the over-all impression of his literary composition. We must also study each unit in the Gospel, as we would study each shell in the vase, to discover what the Holy

Spirit disclosed to the Church - the full meaning of each event and the vital significance of each word in the life of Jesus. "Barnabas M. Ahern, *New Horizons*, (Fides, 1963) 83-84."

The Gospels are not historical documents; nor are they biographies of Jesus. Certainly they do contain some history and some biography but that is not their intent. Rather they are a proclamation of the good news of salvation. The central fact of that proclamation is the narrative of the passion, death, resurrection, and glorification of Jesus. To this central proclamation were added collections of sayings and healings. Still later the infancy narratives were added.

Prior to Vatican II

Prior to Vatican II Catholics had little first hand contact with the Bible. In fact, they were not encouraged to read it. It was the church who told the Catholic faithful what the bible was teaching. Unfortunately "church" here meant simply the hierarchy. They would be the ones who would interpret the scriptures for us. How about the scripture scholars? What was their role? Gone were the days when medieval theologians, like Thomas Aquinas and others, could speak of two magisteriums: the magisterium of the hierarchy and the magisterium of the theologians. (A note: by the way, it was the theologians who did much of the drafting of the documents of Vatican II.!)

I remember when I was in a Catholic grade school we looked forward to Friday, when- if we were good- the teacher would read a Bible story to us. It was not the bible that she read but biblical events presented to us in story form. Thus for many years my contact with the bible was a vicarious contact through stories read in class. I was in my senior year in high school before I owned a bible of my own. Even then I could use only the version approved by church authority.

In the late 19th century and in the years that followed, great strides were made in biblical research by many scholars. Unfortunately, even during the first part of the 20th century the Vatican severely restricted Catholic scholars from involvement in this rapidly growing field of biblical research. Those who involved themselves in anyway were severely censured for the "heresy" of Modernism. George Tyrell, an Irish Jesuit, was excommunicated and expelled from the Jesuits precisely for Modernism. Maude Petre, a friend of Tyrell's, wrote: "The Church lauds those who obey her because they don't care; she punished those who disagree with her because they care." It was a difficult time to be in the Catholic Church and at the same time to be a theologian.

It was not till 1943 that Pius XII, in a landmark encyclical called *Divino Afflante Spiritu,* encouraged Catholic scholars to make appropriate use of modern historical-critical methods of studying the scriptures. (Hurrah for Pius XII who opened the doors for us to understand at last what scripture is all about. I might mention that 1943, was a notable year for another reason. It was the year of my ordination to the priesthood!)

With the door open to contemporary thinking about the Scriptures, Catholics (at least a lot of them) came to understand that the ultimate purpose for reading the scriptures is not to find out the answers to our questions or to obtain theological information; much less to find proof for things we already believe. It is rather to put on the mind of Christ so that we will be able to find answers for our time and our world that reflect God's creating and saving will for all people. Catholic scholars took up the study of the bible with eager enthusiasm.

BIBLICAL AND THEOLOGICAL INSTITUTES

In 1959 an event took place in the archdiocese of Chicago - an event that responded to *Divino Afflante Spiritu*. It was an event that was to be a profound influence on my life and the lives of a lot of other priests. It was the announcement of a Biblical Institute for priests to be held for two weeks in June. I attended the Institute for the first time in 1960 and for at least five years later. While I was there I found out how the Institute came into being. In 1959 Msgr. Daniel Cantwell, Director of Continuing Education for the archdiocese made available for the parishes a booklet on Scripture to be used during Lent. A number of priests came to him and said: "Dan, we can't lead these discussions. We don't know enough about Scripture to lead them." Nothing daunted, Msgr. Cantwell proceeded to put together a Biblical Institute for priests.

The Institute became well known and attracted many priests from many places. I was one of the many who came and by the end of five years I had persuaded a dozen priests from Rochester to join me. During the six years I attended my understanding of scripture changed dramatically from what I had been taught in seminary. It was amazing how Msgr. Cantwell was able to bring in some of the best scripture scholars in the world, including

Raymond Brown, John L. McKenzie, Barnabas Ahern, Gregory Baum and a host of other well known biblical scholars.

The decade of the sixties was a time when biblical and theological institutes sprang up in many places. Besides the Chicago Biblical Institute for priests, I went to similar institutes at various other colleges and universities. In fact, I remember being at an institute at Boston College and chatting with Raymond Brown whom I had come to know at the Chicago Institute. He asked me, laughingly: "Do you go to all these institutes throughout the country?" It was a happy realization for me that I had come to know one of the truly renowned scholars in the field of biblical studies.

Learning to Read the Bible

In the remainder of this chapter I want to explain some of the things that I learned about the Scriptures – and I am concentrating on the Gospels- from the biblical institutes for priests in Chicago and similar institutes elsewhere that I attended. However, I don't want to give all the credit to them. Following the lead given to me in these various institutes, I want – in the rest of this chapter - to draw also from my own study of the scriptures and my personal reflection on them and my regular preaching about them in the liturgy.

The Synoptic Gospels and John

Of the four Gospels it is easy to see that three of them are very similar, namely Matthew, Mark and Luke. They are often referred to as the Synoptic Gospels. They are so called because they correspond so closely with one another that they can be set down in parallel columns; the three of them tell the story of Jesus with different details and emphases. *The various Gospels are each the voices of a living tradition that faithfully bears witness to the truth that the early Christians came to see in Jesus.* The fourth Gospel - which was written sometime after the other three and which differs from them in many respects - very clearly speaks about the gospel writers and the search that their testimony is true.

"Now Jesus did many other signs in the presence of the disciples that are not written in this book. But these are written that you may come to believe that Jesus is the Messiah the son of God, and that through this belief you may have life in his name". (John 20:30).Now I would like to say a few things about each of the Gospels. These are just brief notes about the Gospels that I learned and that I feel are helpful. I would encourage you to let these be just a starting point for your own enquiry into the narrative of each of the Gospels.

MARK   Most scholars now believe that Mark is the oldest Gospel. Matthew and Luke came later and used Mark and some unknown source of Jesus sayings that is simply known as "Q". The funny thing is that we don't have any manuscripts of "Q". It is simply constructed from the Synoptic Gospels and the more than 200 texts that they have in common. Marks's Gospel was the earliest (between AD. 66 to 70). It is also the shortest. As Ronald Witherup says: "it tells the story of Jesus almost breathlessly. Events take place with great speed, one after another. Mark is fond of saying 'and immediately' this or that happened. There is only one instance of Jesus speaking at length, the parable discourse in chapter 4, otherwise Mark describes Jesus as performing miracles and exorcisms." (Witherup, *The Bible Companion* page 174)

Some of the stories he tells are vivid and detailed. This suggests the possibility of contact with eyewitnesses. A long tradition connects this Gospel with St. Peter and the locale of his writing is believed to be Rome. There is a tone of secrecy running through this gospel. No one, not even his chosen disciples, seems to understand who Jesus is or what he is about. Until the end it is only the demons who seem to understand Him.

MATTHEW   The author of Matthew's Gospel was probably a Jewish Christian. Matthew's Gospel has one of the Infancy Narratives the center of which is the visit of the Magi following a star to the birth of a new king. Between the Infancy Narratives and the Passion Narrative, Matthew is made up of five fairly long discourses of Jesus with certain activities and stories in between. These five sections comprise much of the material of this Gospel. The first of these discourses is called the Sermon on the Mount. It begins with the Beatitudes of Jesus. The fact that there are five discourses suggests that Matthew is paralleling Jesus to Moses. Moses gives us the five books which tell us of the law of the people of Israel. Jesus gives us five books telling us of the new law that Jesus brought. These five discourses do indeed suggest Matthew's desire to present Jesus as the new Moses, with the five discourses paralleling the five books of Moses. The fact that the first of these discourses is called "The Sermon on the Mount" further extends the parallel: just as Moses went up the mountain to receive the law from God, so Jesus ascends a mountain to present the

New Law to his people. He is the New Moses giving the New Law.

LUKE   Luke's Gospel is my favorite of the four. It has been called the most beautiful book ever written. From this Gospel we have received the exquisitely beautiful Infancy Narrative that highlights the birth of Jesus in Bethlehem. From this Gospel we have received many memorable scenes that have inspired artists throughout the ages: such as The Annunciation and The Visitation. Indeed the two chapters that cover the Infancy Narratives of Luke have been called the Golden Gospel. The magnificent Chapter Fifteen tells the story of the lost sheep, the lost coin and the lost son. Luke's Gospel narrates, in its Passion - Resurrection Narratives, the beautiful story of the two disciples who met the risen Jesus on their way to their home in Emmaus.

JOHN   The Fourth Gospel came later than the other three, probably written around the year 100. The Fourth Gospel soars above the rest, telling the story of the Word of God become flesh. The Passion Narratives and the multiplication of the loaves and fishes are the only events that John has in common with the other Gospels. Johns' Gospel may be divided into two parts. The first part is called the Book of Signs. What in the other Gospels are seen as miracles, John calls Signs. They are impressive stories in which strong personalities become the vehicle for lengthy discourses of Jesus. The second part is called the Book of Glory; it tells of his return to the Father through his death, resurrection and ascension.

My study and reflection on Scripture played a big role in one of my principal responsibilities as a priest:

namely, preaching the Word of God, especially at the Sunday liturgy. Here are two examples, one of a Sunday homily the other a talk that I gave on the Gospels of Matthew and John.

Example One
The Fifth Sunday of Lent A 2011

What sort of person was this man Lazarus whose story appears so central to today's liturgy? His two sisters, in a message to Jesus, describe him as "the one whom you love." They inform Jesus that Lazarus is ill. Jesus waits two days and comes to Bethany on the third day and raises Lazarus from the dead. Is there a message for us, as we looked toward Easter, in Lazarus being raised from the dead on the third day?

Lazarus appears once more in the Gospel narrative: at the meal where his sister Mary anoints Jesus' feet with precious ointments. He was just there. He never speaks; at least we are not told that he did. How would a man raised from the dead look? What might he have to say? Where would his thoughts be? Robert Browning tried to deal with these intriguing questions in a wonderful poem in which Karshish, a traveling Arab physician, writes to his friend Abib about this man who people claim was raised from the dead. Karshish tells his friend that there is a strangeness about this man. It's as if he is living in two worlds: Heaven opened to a soul while yet on earth; Earth forced on a soul's use while seeing heaven.

Why is this story given to us on this last Sunday of Lent? Perhaps one reason is to confront us with the reality and the inevitability of death: the death of loved ones and, finally, our own death. St. Anselm once expressed a truism: "The farther you are from the time of your birth the closer you are to the time of your death." So many young people think that death is not for them. It is for older people. When we become older people, death's inevitability becomes more real to us. And we are much more earnest about discovering the meaning of death.

Death puts faith to the supreme test. Experience teaches us that there is a finality about death: it ends something: something beautiful, something we prize, something we want to reflect on, as we have reflected on the wonderful lives of our Saint Joseph sisters who have died this year. All that was ended by death. When a loved one dies, death's finality is a fact –an almost brutal fact – that we are forced to face.

Sometimes, when a loved one dies, we accept because we must, but maybe we wish that we could have them with us for a few more years. In the second book of Kings (20) we read of good king Hezekiah. He was mortally ill; he prays for more time. God answers his prayers and adds 15 years to his life. But, in the long run of course, it didn't matter that much. After the 15 years, the finality of death claimed Hezekiah, as it claims all the children of Adam. Remember the solemn words in Gray's "Elegy in a Country Churchyard"?

> The boast of heraldry, the pomp of pow'r,
> And all that beauty, all that wealth e'er gave,
> Await alike the inevitable hour,
> The paths of glory lead but to the grave.

The important question that faith had to deal with is not the finality of death, but whether that finality is also ultimate. For, as Sandra Schneiders has written, "the finality of death lies not in what it terminates, but in what it inaugurates." (Written That You May Believe, 155)

This question: Does death inaugurate something? is answered in today's Gospel, though not in the raising of Lazarus, but in the conversation of Jesus with Martha. Let me explain. Consider Lazarus. In one sense being raised from the dead was for him a wonderful reprieve. He was given a few more years. Yet in another sense, it was no big deal. His life presumably took up where he had left off. Thus if he were forty when he died, he would have returned as a man of forty. If he had died of a heart attack, then he returned to mortal life with a bad heart. He perhaps would live a few more years. Then he had to die again. We might ask the question: "Did he really want to be raised from the dead? Would he have chosen it, had the choice been his? The answer depends on the answer to another question: does death terminate everything; or does death inaugurate something? Does it inaugurate immortal life? If it does, then we can presume that, had he been given the choice, Lazarus would have said: "No thank you" to being raised from the dead. But since it had been done once, he might well have demanded that, the next time he died, a DNR (Do Not Resuscitate) sign be placed at the entrance to his grave. He might also have ordered his sisters: "Keep Jesus away from my tomb."

The raising of Lazarus, then, does not answer the question about the ultimacy of death. It does not answer the question: does death inaugurate something new and wonderful? It is in Jesus' conversation with Martha that these questions find the faith-answer we seek. Martha says to Jesus: "Lord, if you had been here, my brother would not have died. But even now I know that whatever you ask of God, God will give you." Jesus tells her: "Your brother will rise." "I know he will rise in the resurrection on the last day," she responds. Her response indicates that she is thinking about a future a long way off.

Jesus' reply makes clear that he is talking about a future that is present now. For he tells her: "I am the resurrection and the life: whoever believes in me, even if he dies, will live, and everyone who lives and believes in me will never die." Faith in Jesus adds a whole new dimension to our present life. Union with the risen Jesus in this life constitutes the possession, here and now, of eternal life. If we believe in Jesus our present life itself is redolent with eternal life.

As we reflect on this Gospel narrative, suddenly the stage changes. It is no longer Jesus speaking to Martha, but to each of us. Each of us has to hear Jesus' question: "Do you believe this?" At this point believing becomes not theological assent, but a spiritual transformation that is deeply personal. It is not something that we can prove (indeed we have no desire even to think at that level). Believing in Jesus is experiencing Jesus as the Risen One. It's accepting Him. It's saying "Yes" to him as the one who gives us life, immortal, unending life.

Faith in this respect is like love. Love can't be proved either (you wouldn't even want to think of love at that level). It's like living in a family or a community and discovering that love is there. You receive it. You experience it. You return it. And it makes life worthwhile.

It is living faith in Jesus, living faith in his resurrection, living faith in his incorporating us into his risen life that assures us that, no matter how real and no matter how depriving it may seem, death is temporary and passing, for it has been overcome by Jesus' resurrection.

This is the faith we share. It is this faith that makes it so important that we belong to community, that we belong to the Church. For belonging to the Church means, in ultimate terms, being united in a community of Easter people, who believe that Jesus was raised from the dead, who believe that he lives eternally and, therefore, believe him when he says that he gives us eternal life. Stripped down to its basic essentials, that is what Church is: a community of Easter people. Recently Dr. Rowan Williams, archbishop of Canterbury, defined Church as "what happens when people encounter the risen Christ" and commit themselves to "sustaining and deepening that encounter" with others. We face death unflinchingly, for we have the assurance of faith that it inaugurates something most wonderful: immortal life in God.

Example Two

Contrasting Two Gospels

(Talk I gave at a convocation of the deacons and their wives at the diocese of Rochester, New York)

I need to point out that each of the Gospels has its own distinctive character and intent. Let me give a fairly detailed example. Contrasting the Gospel of Matthew with that of John, it quickly becomes apparent that Matthew is the most ecclesiastical of the Gospels and John the least. In fact, the word "church" appears only twice in the four Gospels, both times in Matthew. There is the well-known passage, in chapter 16, about Peter as the Rock on which the Church will be built; and in chapter 18 the description of the procedure for correcting an erring brother or sister. Three steps are outlined: first you speak to the erring person one on one; if that doesn't work, you go with 2 or 3 others; finally, if the erring one still remains obstinate, you refer the matter to the Church. Reading Matthew, one soon becomes aware that the church of Matthew was a structured, hierarchical community with authority quite clearly defined.

Moving from Matthew to John, you find yourself entering a completely different ecclesial world. The community of the 4th Gospel is strongly egalitarian. No hierarchy is mentioned, no structure described. The emphasis in the Johannine community is on the relation of the individual Christian to Jesus Christ. I should point out, though, that the 4th Gospel offers no justification for a "Jesus and me" spirituality or a "Jesus as my personal savior" mentality. No, the sense of community, expressed in such metaphors as the vine and the branches, the shepherd and the sheep, is very strong. Coupled with this healthy awareness of community is the strong consciousness that the source of direction in the community lies not in a structured hierarchy, but in the Spirit, who both replaces Jesus and at the same time makes him present. It is the Spirit who leads the community into the truth. The Spirit is the Spirit of truth and of love. What distinguishes the community is the love the members have for one another.

If Peter is the hero of Matthew's Gospel, that role in the 4th Gospel belongs to a mysterious person who is not named, but who is called "the disciple whom Jesus loved" or "the Beloved Disciple." Significantly, the term "apostle" never appears in the 4th Gospel. There is no doubt that the author of the 4th Gospel knew of the apostles (he does refer to the "Twelve"), but the distinguishing status in the Johannine Church is not apostleship, but discipleship. And it is a discipleship of equals who are loved by Jesus and who strive to love one another as he has loved them. The model, though not the leader, of the community, is "the Beloved Disciple." It is true that Peter's position of leadership is recognized in the 4th Gospel, as in the other three. Still he must yield prominence to the Beloved Disciple. Thus, though in the other Gospels Peter appears as spokesperson for the Twelve, he cannot, in the 4th Gospel, speak directly to Jesus at the supper banquet of love; he can only address Jesus through the intermediary of the Beloved Disciple. In the Synoptic tradition, Peter, while following Jesus into the court of the high priest, in the end denies Jesus and abandons him, as had the rest. The lone male disciple who stands at the foot of the cross is the Beloved Disciple.

And on Easter morn, when Peter and the Beloved Disciple run to the tomb, it is only the Beloved Disciple who believes without seeing Jesus. Then a few days later, when the disciples have gone fishing with Peter and a Stranger speaks to them from the shore, it is the Beloved Disciple who recognizes the Stranger and says: "It is the

Lord." Even when office is recognized as a practical pastoral necessity (obviously there must be some kind of leadership in the community), the holder of office must pass the test of the Johannine community. Peter is given the role of shepherding in the name of Jesus, but it is a role that must be based, not on power, but on love. That is why, before the bestowal of office, Peter has to declare, three times (!), his love for Jesus. Even then the sheep still belong to Jesus. And Peter must follow in the footsteps of the Good Shepherd: he must be ready to lay down his life for the sheep. A particularly significant testimony to the egalitarian character of the Johannine Church is the attitude it shows toward women. There are narratives in the 4th Gospel about strong women: for instance, the Samaritan woman, Mary and Martha. In the depiction and development of character and personality, their stories show them as equal in importance to the important men, such as the blind man and Lazarus. Then there is the profession of faith which the Synoptics place on the lips of Peter ("You are the Christ, the Son of the living God") that becomes in the Johannine community the profession of Martha, who says: "You are the Christ, the Son of God." And on Easter morn it is not Peter, but Mary Magdalene who is the first to see the risen Jesus and announce the Easter proclamation: "I have seen the Lord." This unique role wins for her the dignity of being the *apostola apostolorum*. Clearly, it is love for Jesus, not gender, that makes for equality in the community of the Beloved Disciple. Such a community could never have agreed with the pastoral epistles, with 1 Timothy 2:12, for instance, where the writer says: "I do not permit a woman to teach or to have authority over a man; rather she must be silent."

Such an attitude would run quite foreign to the egalitarian thinking of the community of the Beloved Disciple.

From what I have suggested, ever so briefly, one can see that Matthew and John embody ecclesiologies markedly different from one another. Matthean ecclesiology is distinctly hierarchical: there are divinely appointed teachers whose task is to teach, admonish and instruct the rest of the members of the church.

Such an ecclesiology, standing all by itself, can easily become rigid and inflexible. Failure to tap the resources of truth and understanding in rest of the ecclesial body can mean the loss of valuable insights and intuitions that exist among the faithful. A one-sided emphasis on Matthean ecclesiology could mean (and in the history of the church oftentimes has meant) the stifling of the Spirit who dwells in all God's people.

The much more attractive Johannine ecclesiology, on the other hand, also has its shortcomings. The belief that the Spirit is present as a living divine teacher in the heart of every disciple is surely one of the great contributions to Christian faith made by the 4th Gospel. Yet at the same time it can easily become a source of chaos, confusion and instability. What happens when disciples who have the Spirit disagree with one another? As Raymond Brown says: "Johannine ecclesiology is the most attractive and exciting in the NT. Alas it is also one of the least stable."

Matthean ecclesiology makes for stability, but with a tendency toward rigidity; Johannine ecclesiology is much more flexible, but easily leads to instability and lack of harmony. The ideal would be to combine the two; and it is the genius of the Church Catholic that it accepted into its canon of scripture, not Matthew alone, not John alone, but both Matthew and John. For this we can be grateful.

****

Above is the talk that I delivered to the deacons and their wives. Now I would like to reflect further on the content of that talk.

It would be wonderful if the best of these two approaches to the church could be combined with one another in congenial and harmonious wedlock. Yet, as we turn the pages of history, it becomes evident that efforts to wed the two have scarcely ever resulted in a perfect marriage. I am reminded of the story of George Bernard Shaw. A young woman known for her beauty, but not her intelligence, once said to Shaw: "Imagine what a wonderful child we could have: with your mind and my body." "True," he agreed, "but there is another possibility: what if the child had my body and your brains"?

An ecclesiology of authority has scarcely ever lived comfortably with an understanding of church in which there is an equality of disciples, each led and directed by the Spirit of God. There will always be Matthean Christians who will maintain that the only portal through which the Spirit can enter the church is the hierarchy. All the living impulses in the church, they would maintain, originate in its official ministers.

Yet the Johannine ecclesial insight is there, enshrined in the 4th Gospel. It insists that there is another impulse of the Spirit operating in the church. Beside the impulse from the Spirit operating in the hierarchy, there are also stirrings of the Spirit that are experienced by and originate in, the people of God who are outside the hierarchy.

Stirrings of The Spirit In The Church

Allowing for this double stirring of the Spirit in the Church will inevitably mean a certain amount of untidiness that would of course be absent if the only vehicle used by the Spirit were to be the hierarchy. Indeed, not only untidiness, but disparate and opposed tendencies and trends may appear. As Karl Rahner has said: "When various influences flow from God into the Church, some through ministry, others directly to members of the Church who hold no office, it is clear that God alone can clearly perceive the meaning, direction and divinely willed purpose of these." Rahner goes on to say that ultimately there is only one thing that can give unity to the Church at the human level and that is love, "which allows another to be different, even when it does not understand him [or her]." It is love that the Johannine ecclesiology would pump into the Church in abundance.

When church authority canonizes one particular trend in theology, it does a disservice to the Church. Rahner suggests that a glance into history will make clear to us that there has never been a theological trend in the Church that has been wholly and solely right and has triumphed over all others. Every theological trend in the Church has moved at best toward "magnetic north," never toward "true north." In Rahner's words: "One alone has always been completely right, the one Lord who, one in himself, has willed the many opposing tendencies in the Church." Realizing this frees one from anxiety and from the need always to be right.

The Everywhereness Of The Risen Jesus

It may well be that the only feasible way of dealing with such tensions is to turn to the one who is at the center of the reality we call Church – the Risen Jesus who is ever in our midst. The Jesus of history was mortal. He could die – and he did die. The Risen One, on the other hand, can never die. He is totally in God who is all life. This says to us that Jesus, the Risen One, is freed from the limitation of particularities. In his mortal life he was limited by the particularities of time, geography, culture and gender. In his Risen Life the limitations of particularity are removed. Jesus is no longer confined by our world of time and space, yet he is at the same time very much with us. The Risen One is everywhere. He belongs to all history and to all peoples. He is the contemporary of every age. He is our contemporary. He is ever in our midst. [Now I must warn the reader that I have slipped into a bit of Chapter 2, but I am sure you will not mind because that chapter is coming soon. Please forgive me. But after all I am the author of this book and can write what I choose to write. The only drawback for me, however, is that you may choose whether you read this or not. So I go on.]

The everywhereness of the risen Jesus is the core reality of our spirituality. That is what contemplation is all about: being aware that He is there. For He is indeed everywhere. He comes to us in hidden, sometimes subversive ways. He breaks through into our lives and our history in surprising and unsuspected ways. We are never really prepared for Him. He is in the person to whom you gave a helping hand today. He is in the harried cashier at Wegmans who takes your money, in the nurse who takes your blood pressure, in the pharmacist who dispenses the many pills we take.

And he is in Iraq and Afghanistan with our courageous service men and women and with the suffering people in those countries. He is with the countless number of the poor and homeless in so many of our own cities and in the rural areas of our country: people who often have to make a choice between food and medicine. He dwells amidst the thousands of people in the Sudan who die because they have no food or medicine.

He is in those people in our world and in our midst who are homeless, sick, dying, discriminated against. The forgotten people of the world. He is in them reproaching us when we ignore their plight. Indeed, He is everywhere -- and the world is never quite ready for Him. Sadly, so often it doesn't realize his presence, maybe doesn't even want it. But any effort to confine the Christ, to limit His Presence, is doomed to failure. There is no escaping Him. He is beyond our control.

He energizes His Church, leading it and always going on before it even into areas where, for the moment at least, the Church is afraid to venture. Always a step ahead of us. Always beckoning us to new horizons we have not yet reached. Especially today – as we face conflict and even panic in the Church such as we have never experienced before – we need to see him so far ahead of us, beckoning us onward. He is the lover of the Song of Songs, springing across the mountains, leaping across the hills. He gazes through the windows, peering through the lattices. A lover, He calls us to love: to love Him and to love the believing and the unbelieving world He came to save and in which he dwells.

Passion and Resurrection

Finally, returning to this brief survey of what I have learned about Scripture, I need to speak about the passion and death of Jesus – the event that climaxed in the earth-shaking event of His resurrection. It is important to see these events as forming a single unit, that, taken together constitute the foundation of Christian faith. It is essential to realize that without the resurrection the passion and death of Jesus would be of little significance for us. The resurrection is **that** important. I emphasize this truth because for many years the resurrection was not given its rightful place in the scheme of salvation.

It is also important to point out that the way we have come to know the climactic event of the resurrection is because Jesus Himself revealed it to us. Had he not appeared to his disciples in the upper room or to the two disciples on the way to Emmaus or to whomever else he may have appeared, we would never have known about the resurrection. Jesus of Nazareth would have passed through the pages of history without any one knowing the story of this world-changing event.

During the first millennium, it was the resurrection that dominated Christian thinking about redemption. As I mentioned earlier this is clearly expressed in St. Paul's first epistle to the Corinthians where, in Chapter 15, he says;

"I handed down to you as of first importance what I also received: that Christ died for our sins in accordance with the Scriptures, that he was buried, that he was raised on the third day in accordance with the Scriptures, that he appeared to Kephas, then to the Twelve. After that, he appeared to more than 500 brothers at once, most of whom are still living though some have fallen asleep. After that he appeared to James then to all the apostles. Last of all as to one born abnormally, He appeared to me."

This is Paul's witness to the reality of the resurrection. This is Paul's list of those to whom Jesus appeared after His resurrection.

Take a moment to reflect on those whom Paul might have listed as the ones to whom Jesus appeared. Or we might put the matter another way; to whom might we expect Jesus to appear?

Certainly he had ample opportunities to dispel all doubts about the truth of His resurrection. Thus, for instance, He could have appeared in Pilate's palace, perhaps when Pilate and his wife were having breakfast. That would have set the whole Roman world a-wondering. Pilate's wife could have said to her husband afterwards: "I told you to have nothing to do with this man."

Or Jesus might have suddenly turned up at a meeting of the Sanhedrin and forced them by the pure evidence of his presence to accept the fact that a man whom they knew for certain had died was now, inexplicably, but beyond any shadow of doubt, alive.

Another possibility would have been even more dramatic; He could have had his followers organize a procession like the one held on Palm Sunday. He could have ridden into Jerusalem, mounted this time not on a lowly donkey but on a great horse- the kind of horse that today could win the Kentucky Derby- and greet people as he rode triumphantly through the city. Yes, these are the kind of appearances that would have silenced all doubt.

An even better idea: why didn't he appear to Tiberius Caesar in Rome? He could have ordered the emperor to proclaim the Gospel throughout the empire. This would have meant that the empire would have become Christian some 300 years before the time of Constantine. Think of how much easier things would have been all around, if Jesus had done this. All those bloody martyrdoms would have been spared. Peter would not have had to die upside down on the cross. Paul wouldn't have had to have his head chopped off at the *Tre Fontane* outside the city of Rome. Ignatius of Antioch and Perpetua and Felicity and Agnes and Cecelia and so many others would not have been thrown to wild beasts in the Roman Coliseum.

If Jesus had made these types of appearances, non-believers would be overwhelmed by the evidence.

Yet these are precisely the kind of things that Jesus did not do. He appeared to no one except those who were disposed to believe. There is an intriguing statement in the 10th Chapter of *Acts of the Apostles* that calls for a serious reflection, if we are to understand the meaning of the resurrection and what it means to accept the resurrection.

In *Acts 10* Peter goes to Caesarea to the home of the Roman Centurion, Cornelius, who was interested in hearing more about Jesus. Peter preached what was clearly the proclamation of the early disciples of Jesus; "How God anointed Jesus of Nazareth with the Holy Spirit and power, how He went about doing good and healing all who were oppressed by the devil for God was with him."

Peter then proceeds to clarify for Cornelius and for us the important role of the disciples of Jesus. He says, "We are witnesses to all he had done both in Judea and Jerusalem. They put him to death by hanging him upon a tree: but God raised him on the third day and allowed him to appear, **not to all the people, but to us** who were chosen by God as witnesses, and who ate and drank with him after he rose from the dead. (Acts 10;38-41).

There is the real clincher! God allowed him to appear not to all the people, but as Peter says, "to us who were chosen by God as witnesses and who shared meals with Him after He rose from the dead." Evidently God allowed the risen Jesus to be seen only by those who were linked to Him by some bond of love and friendship. Those who didn't know Him and those who opposed Him during his mortal life simply never got to see Him as the Risen One.

Now could this mean that the risen Jesus just never got around to see anyone except His close followers? Clearly there is more than that in this text from *Acts*; it wasn't just that these people didn't see him, because it happened that their paths never crossed. No, it is something deeper. Peter does not simply say that these people did not see Him. He is clearly implying - at least this is what I think- that they *could not see Him*. Let me make this very concrete. Recall the Easter Sunday night meeting of Jesus with his disciples when he appeared to them in the upper room. Suppose that a member of the Sanhedrin or an officer in Pilate's court had been able to sneak into the room unobserved. Jesus appears. Would such a person have seen Him? I think not. This seems to me to be the meaning of Peter's words where he says Jesus appeared not to all the people but only to us who had been chosen to be witnesses.

Interestingly, St. Thomas Aquinas discussed this matter. He says that it was only Jesus' disciples who recognized him as risen because of the discerning power of faith. This is my translation of a Latin term used by Thomas. He says only these witnesses saw Jesus after his death because they saw Him alive *"Oculata fide."* Oculus is the Latin word for "eye". *"Oculata fide"* means faith that has eyes. It is something like the "third eye" spoken of in Eastern religions. Anyway, I have translated it as the discerning power of faith. The disciples may have lost hope in Jesus after He died, but they never lost their love for Him and their faith in Him. And it was this love and faith that gave them the discerning eye that enabled them to recognize Him when others could not.

One final point I want to make about the resurrection. Seeing the risen Jesus was not an experience of empirical data; it was experience of faith. For the very best empirical experience might have achieved was an experience of resuscitation not resurrection.

Recall the story of Lazarus. He was mortal and he died. He was resuscitated and therefore was living again, but even after his resuscitation he was still mortal. Hence people could see him before and after because in both cases he was mortal: and therefore the subject of empirical data even after his resuscitation.

The mortal Jesus -the Jesus before his death- could like the mortal Lazarus, have been experienced as a fact of empirical data. The Risen Jesus, however, could only be experienced by faith. For resurrection is not returning from the dead it is a leap beyond death to a totally different kind of existence. Such a leap cannot be empirically verified. Therefore the resurrection does not mean that Jesus' mortal life had been prolonged. No, his life after the resurrection was completely different from the life he had lived for more than three decades among his family, friends, and followers. That is the intriguing puzzle that the resurrection stories make evident to us: clearly, after the resurrection, He was the same Jesus they had known and followed; they recognized His voice, they touched Him, they shared meals with Him. The Gospels very definitely emphasize the physical character of His appearances.

Yet equally the Gospels make clear that there was something bewilderingly different about the risen Jesus. He was no longer subject to the limitation that mortality places upon us (And indeed placed on Him too before His resurrection). Thus, once risen, he could be present to his friends, without their recognizing him. He could enter rooms where the doors were shut. He could appear suddenly and just as suddenly disappear as he did with the two disciples with whom he broke bread at Emmaus. Yes, it was the same Jesus but what a difference!

As Frank P. De Siano, CSP has written: "The defining moment for those who have faith in Jesus Christ is the resurrection. Without the resurrection of Jesus we are simply on a nostalgic trip, remembering a great historical figure who spoke powerfully and meaningfully. But ultimately, as St. Paul insisted, our faith without the resurrection, is foolish and empty."

During most of the first millennium, it was the resurrection, not the crucifixion, that was at the heart of Christian faith. Indeed the crucifixion of Jesus was initially something of an embarrassment for the early church. The reason: a passage from the book of Deuteronomy which placed a curse on the person hanging on a tree as a punishment for a capital offense. In Chapter 3 of the Epistle to the Galatians Paul says; "Christ ransomed us from the curse of the law by becoming a curse for us, for it is written, cursed be every one who hangs on a tree." The reference is to Deuteronomy Chapter 21 which says; "If a man guilty of a capital offense is put to death and his corpse hung on a tree, it shall not remain on the tree overnight. You shall bury it the same day; otherwise, since God's curse rests on him who hangs on a tree, you will defile the land which the Lord your God is giving you as an inheritance."

It was during the Middle Ages that devotion to the sufferings and death of Jesus came into prominence as a devotional practice. It gradually replaced the resurrection as the center of Christian faith and spirituality. The devotion of the Stations of the Cross became very popular. It was a reflection on various scenes of the passion, as Jesus made his way from the place of judgment to Mt. Golgotha, where he died the excruciating death of crucifixion. The way of the cross was first a devotional practice in the Holy Land. When it became impossible to go to the Holy Land

Christians began to set up stations in their own lands. Remembering the passion of Jesus in a number of stations became widespread in the Christian world. Many of you who remember the church before Vatican II will recall that during Lent the devotion of the Stations of the Cross was held every Friday evening. Indeed for many people this was a popular devotion to carry out at any time they wished. It was not unusual to go to church and see someone walking about the church and pausing for prayer at each of the fourteen stations depicting the passion story from the judgment by Pilate to the death of Jesus. In recent years some people have wanted to add a fifteenth station commemorating the resurrection.

This devotion – to Jesus suffering and death - was a wonderful development in Christian spirituality, but – unfortunately - it led to a down-grading of the resurrection as the foundational truth of Christian faith. St. Thomas Aquinas, for instance, saw the resurrection not as a salvific event but as a reward that God gave to Jesus for undergoing His passion. In my own time the resurrection was thought of as the *crowning proof of the divinity of Christ*. In fact, in my "unenlightened years" (the time before my "Conversions"), I wrote a book called *The Church of Christ*. Much of what I wrote there I now solemnly repudiate. If you have a copy of it, I beg you burn it. One of the chapters presents a detailed discussion of the resurrection as the crowning proof that Jesus was truly God.

Later in my own time the resurrection was reestablished as the pivotal, decisive point of redemption. For this we can all be grateful to F.X. Durwell and his book

The Resurrection of Christ for this return to an understanding of the resurrection that existed in the early days of the church. Father Durwell's book reaffirmed the earliest teaching of the church that the resurrection was the pivotal point of Christian faith and spirituality. This had a number of effects in the life of the church. Thus, in 1955 Pope Pius XII permitted a return to the Easter vigil as a solemn celebration.

I can remember yesteryears when on Palm Sunday the priest would announce that the service of Holy Saturday would begin at seven o'clock. At that time the priest would read all of the lessons for Holy Saturday. He also told the congregation that the Mass would begin about eight o'clock and they might as well wait till then to come for the Holy Saturday service. Indeed it can probably be said that in those days Lent ended on Good Friday when the passion of Jesus was remembered. Then on Saturday morning we would wait for the clock to strike 12, the time that we would be able to give up our Lenten penances. Easter Sunday was another big celebration, though it was not seen as a part of the Easter Triduum with little connection to the services of Holy Saturday.

This restoration of a solemn celebration of the Easter vigil led to a whole new understanding of the liturgical year. Easter, as a celebration of the resurrection of Jesus, became the high point of that year. Christmas is surely an important celebration in the liturgical year; but without the resurrection Christmas would have no special importance for us. The resurrection is ***that*** important.

The Infancy Narratives

We have discussed the resurrection narratives that bring the Gospel story to a smashing conclusion: a marvelous ending, which is not really an ending at all, but the beginning of something totally and wonderfully new. For in the resurrection humanity in Jesus takes on immortality.

Now I would like to write a brief account of what the Gospels tell us about the beginning of the mortal existence of Jesus. I should point out at once that the story of Jesus' infancy is narrated in only two of the Gospels, namely, Luke and Matthew. Even more important: **it must also be noted that the infancy narratives are *not* part of the apostolic witness.** This is clearly stated by Peter in the earliest days at a gathering of the disciples of Jesus after the Ascension, in which he lays down the conditions for choosing a successor to Judas as one of the 12. (See *Acts* 1:21:22) "It is necessary that one of the men who accompanied us, beginning from the baptism of John until the day on which he was taken up from us, become with us a witness to his resurrection."

You will note that Peter is asserting that the apostolic witness begins with the time of the baptism of Jesus by John. This certainly suggests that the original disciples of Jesus did not know the details of his birth and early upbringing.

Comparing The Infancy Narratives Of Matthew And Luke

The infancy narratives in Matthew and Luke differ not only from the main body of the Gospel material but they differ significantly from one another.

There are certain points of agreement between them
1. Jesus was born during the reign of Herod the Great;
2. Born in Bethlehem, but brought up in Nazareth;
3. His mother was Mary, a virgin at the time of Jesus birth;
4. Jesus was conceived through the activity of the Holy Spirit;
5. Mary's husband was Joseph;
6. Jesus was named at the command of an angel.

There are certain points of disagreement:
1. The residence of Mary and Joseph in Matthew is Bethlehem; in Luke it is Nazareth;
2. Luke knows nothing about Herod and all Jerusalem being upset. Nor does he know of the Magi and the star and the flight into Egypt, and Herod's slaughter of the infants;
3. Matthew knows nothing about to the census nor of the appearance of the shepherds.

They also shared a tendency to dramatize and homilize their Christology against the background of Old Testament stories and texts. They meditate on these sacred texts and present an imaginative reconstruction of them. They tell us often in homiletic, story form the truth summed up by John:" and the word became flesh and lived among us. We have seen His glory the glory as of the Father's only Son, full of grace and truth." (Jn. 1:14).The

Infancy Narratives, therefore, should not be read as history, but as reflections on Old Testament texts or early Christian experiences. For example, in Luke, it is stated that there is no room in the inn. This may be seen as evoking God's complaint against Israel in *Isaiah* 1: 3 "The ass knows his master and the donkey knows the manger of his Lord, but Israel has not known me."An example from Matthew; the narrative of the flight into Egypt. It speaks of Herod ordering the death of the children of Bethlehem. This is very similar to the action of the Pharaoh who tried to destroy the infant Moses. Herod is also like Balac, king of the Moabites who tried to get Balaam the soothsayer to curse the Israelites. Instead a blessing comes from his mouth. See Numbers: 24:17; "Oracle of Balaam whose eye is clear… who hears the word of God;

> "I see him but not now
> I behold him but not near
> A star comes out of Jacob
> and a scepter shall rise out of Israel."

This could well be the star that led the Magi to the Child.

    Efforts have been made to harmonize the two infancy narratives in Matthew and Luke. It just will not work. They are two different stories. Trying to harmonize the two is like taking two different jig-saw puzzles of the same place or event and trying to fit them together. These stories should be left and enjoyed as the beautiful stores [stories] they are.

Praying with the Scriptures

    The Second Vatican Council in its decree on Revelation has said; "Let it never be forgotten that prayer should accompany the reading of holy scripture, so that it becomes a dialogue between God and the human reader, for "when we pray, we talk to God; when we read the divine word we listen to him. " One form of praying with scripture is the very ancient practice, called Lectio Divina. Literally Lectio Divina means "Divine Reading" or "Holy Reading." Thomas Merton suggests that it is called divine, "Because it calls to mind divine truths and prolongs itself in prayer with God." Generally lectio is reading the scriptures. It means a slow contemplative praying of the scriptures. This enables the bible, the word of God, to become a way of union with God. This approach to prayer has a long history in Christian spirituality.

It involves four steps 1) Reading "Lectio", 2) Meditation "Mediatio", 3) Prayer "With words" "Oratio" , 4) Contemplation "Contemplatio." This approach to prayer – it goes back to the desert Fathers in the early church- was put into words by Guigo II (died 1188), the ninth prior of the Grand Chartreuse in a work called *Scala claustralium* (the ladder of monks). The image recalls the biblical story in which Jacob saw a ladder reaching from earth to heaven (Genesis 28:10-19). Guigo's ladder has just four rungs. Reading is thoughtful slow reflective perusing of the scripture text. Meditation involves repeating the text; ruminating (chewing) on the text. Prayer is the turning toward God in words of praise thanks sorrow and petition. Contemplation is God's gift to us enabling us to experience God directly beyond words and concepts.

It is interesting to note the ways in which Guigo relates the four steps to one another. In the case of the first three his says that one sends you to the other. (The Latin word he uses is *mittit*). But step four is different. Thus, while reading sends you to meditation and meditation sends you to (Vocal) prayer, prayer does not send you to contemplation. Contemplation is different from the other rungs of the ladder. It is in a class by itself. The first three are about things we can do. Contemplation is what God does. Thus, when he introduces it, Guigo simply says "contemplation when it comes takes us out of our realm of doing and enables us simply to be in the presence of God." Thomas Merton writes in *New Seeds of Contemplation* "Contemplation reaches out to the knowledge and even the experience of the transcendent and inexpressible God. It knows God by seeming to touch him or rather it knows him as if it had been invisibly touched by him… Touched by Him who has no hands, but is pure Reality and the source of all that is real! Hence contemplation is a sudden gift of awareness, an awakening to the Real within all that is real.

AN EXERCSE IN CONTEMPLATIVE PRAYER

Some Suggestions

1. Find a time - a half hour and at regular time each day, if possible - during which you can be silent and quiet. Sometimes such an atmosphere may not be entirely possible and we simply do the best we can.

2. In order to quiet the mind and heart, take a few deep breaths, inhaling the air that is fresh and clear and exhaling the musty and the stale. Then say a brief prayer; "Help me to live in your presence."

3. Gently but firmly let go of words and thoughts (even those about God), also let go of cares, concerns, and anxieties (at least for this brief period of time).

4. Try just to be quiet, knowing in faith that you are in the presence of God, which means being in the presence of love. Just relax in this silence of the divine presence. Just be there. Do not feel that there is anything that you have to do.

5. If you are distracted (as surely you will be), quietly let go of the distractions to the degree that you can. If they remain or return, don't be disturbed; for you are still in the presence of God. To deal with the distractions, you might want to repeat the brief prayer (given above) to help you return to inner quiet and silence. But don't fuss too much about distraction.

6. Conclude with the Lord's Prayer or a favorite psalm or some spontaneous words of praise and thanks.

7. Try to develop the habit of saying a brief prayer at different times during the day. This is a way of keeping awareness of God closer to the surface of consciousness.

Here are three short prayers that can be used:

(a) Help me to live in your presence

(b) Help me to experience the joy of your presence

(c) I will walk in the presence of the Lord in the land of the living

    Thomas Merton wrote; "I have a very simple way of prayer. It is centered entirely on attention to the presence of God and to His will and His love." (We shall discuss more about Merton's way of prayer in Chapter Two).

    This is but a preview of what is to come.

CHAPTER TWO
THOMAS MERTON AND A NEW WAY OF UNDERSTANDING PRAYER

"The Christian of the future either will be a mystic or no Christian at all."
-Karl Rahner, T.I. 20, 149

This year, 2010, marks the 42nd anniversary of the death of Thomas Merton. It is also the 67th anniversary of his best selling autobiography, *The Seven Storey Mountain*. In the time stretching between these two events, Merton managed to produce a body of literature staggering in its size and impressive in its prophetic vision. Among other things his writings have helped to charter a new path for American Catholic Spirituality.

Merton hardly thought of this as his role. In an interview given to Thomas P. McDonnell in 1968 Merton insisted on his right not to be turned into a Catholic myth for children in parochial schools. He could not abide the thought that anyone would set him up as an ideal to be honored or as a model to be imitated. That same year a young man wrote to him saying he wanted to come to Gethsemani because he had been strongly attracted to Merton through his writings. Merton's advice to him was to pray and seek God's will. But don't, he said, "build on a mud pile like me! I just don't have disciples, don't look for disciples, and don't think I could be of any use to disciples. My suggestion to you is to be a disciple of Christ, and not of any man."

Whether he liked it or not Thomas Merton has been the spiritual director of ever so many people who have found that the spirituality they discovered in his writings offered a *new way of life for them*. It reshaped their spirituality.

Teaching a Course on Thomas Merton

It shaped mine also. The next conversion experience I want to talk about, therefore, is my coming to a new way of thinking about prayer. This experience came through my study, reading, and writing about Thomas Merton. It was from him that the word contemplation came to take on a meaning for me that it had never had before. The way in which I came to this new understanding is worth recording. I was moved to a deeper involvement in Merton's writings by two students. They were taking a course in Catholic studies that I was teaching at Nazareth College in Rochester, New York. At one point in the course I quoted a brief text from Thomas Merton. These two students came to me and asked that I teach a course on Merton. I was reluctant at first, and then finally gave in to their request. And I was hooked.

The course was given in the summer of 1974. As I prepared to teach this course and as I taught it for them and a dozen other students who had signed up for it, it gradually struck me that Merton had given me this wonderful gift that I have already spoken of, namely a new approach to prayer and spirituality. It's an approach I would like to call "contemplative spirituality." I would say that this was a gift that he gave not only to me (and, hopefully), to the students who took this course, (or at least some of them). Indeed it was a gift to the whole Christian community. I say it was his gift not because he invented it, but because he rescued it from the marginal position it had for so long a time occupied in Catholic life. He placed it at the center of our understanding of spirituality. Thomas Merton's greatest achievement, I believe, was to help us understand that contemplation was not just for monks. He made contemplation a household word.

Teaching this course, combined with more and more reading of Merton's books, did indeed open my mind to a completely new way of thinking about what it means to pray.

At this time in my life I truly needed to come to such an understanding. I would not have been able to describe my prayer life or if I did it would have been an understanding of prayer that did not satisfy me. As a young priest I went to a Roman Catholic seminary and I presumed that there I would learn how to pray. After all, I felt that one of the things I would be expected to do as a priest would be to help people to learn how to pray. After the first year of seminary, I had not yet learned how to pray. But I figured it would happen the following year. But it didn't happen then either; and the same fate marked the next four years. So I was ordained a priest and felt somewhat like a phony because I really didn't know how to pray or at least I didn't think I knew how to pray.

An Insight

But, after teaching this course on Merton I continued reading what Merton had to say about prayer and contemplation. This helped me to understand a text from St. Paul's epistle to the Romans that had always puzzled me: "The spirit comes to the aid of our weakness for *we do not know how to pray* as we ought, but the spirit itself intercedes with inexpressible groanings and the one who searches hearts knows what is the intention of the spirit because it intercedes for the holy ones according to God's will." (Romans 8:26-27)

I had read this text many times without really understanding what it meant. Suddenly my eyes were opened, and I realized what Paul was saying. In effect he was telling me to let go of my desire to pray and let God pray in me! Just be attentive to and aware of God's presence. The spirit who lives in me will do the praying. The thunderbolt that hit me was the understanding that I needed to be silent and let prayer happen in me. For so long a time I had thought that I could not pray and all that time prayer had been happening in me! What I needed most was to quiet down and be truly aware of what was going on in me and let it happen. This was a wonderful insight that brought peace to me. I suspect, however, that such an insight might not have come to me if I had not, at the same time been deeply immersed in what Thomas Merton had to say about prayer (and about a lot of other things too).

Experiences that Led to Deeper Involvement

A number of providential events led to an almost inevitable involvement in further Merton studies. In the very year that I taught this course on Merton, I was traveling with a friend on vacation and the first stop of our vacation was Louisville, Kentucky. My companion, Father Edward Lintz, went there to preside at a wedding ceremony. Since I was not interested in staying for the wedding, I decided to go to the Abbey of Gethsemani which was only about 40 miles away. When I arrived there I met Brother Patrick Hart who had been Thomas Merton's secretary. He greeted me most cordially and took me to visit Merton's Hermitage. This was the beginning of a friendship that still continues.

The year following my visit to Gethsemani brought me to Indianapolis for a meeting of the College Theology Society. After the meeting I drove to Louisville to examine the Merton collection at Bellarmine College. There began another long-term friendship, -this one with the late Robert Daggy, curator of the Merton collection. From that time on, my visits to Gethsemani and to the Merton Center at Bellarmine College became as frequent as I could manage.

The three of us, Brother Patrick, Bob Daggy, and I were very much involved in bringing to birth the International Thomas Merton Society. In the beginning there were 14 members the first meeting was held in Louisville in 1989 with more than 100 attending. Since then meetings have been held every two years. The society has chapters in many areas of the United States, but also in Europe and the Far East.

An Interesting Letter

Frequently I receive letters from people with a wide variety of backgrounds who tell me that their lives have been profoundly influenced by Merton. For instance, recently I received a letter from a woman in the southwest who told me how Thomas Merton had changed her life. Now in her 50th year she wrote that she had grown up during a period in the church in which lay people were considered second-class members. The spirituality that had guided her (and me too, for all too long) was a devotional spirituality.

She wrote: "Thomas Merton was the one who provided a breakthrough for me. It came in a section of *The Seven Storey Mountain* in which he speaks of the contemplative vocation as one to which all are called. It was the first time in my adult life," (she continued) "in which the guilt of not following a religious vocation fell away and I had permission-from my own spirit-to continue my journey to wholeness as a lay person."

Reflect for a moment on what she said about the way in which Merton transformed her understanding of spirituality. *First*, it freed her from a terrible guilt feeling: the feeling that because she had not followed a call to religious life she had deliberately chosen an inferior way of living her Christian vocation. (This was a widespread attitude among most Catholics)

Second, Merton taught her that her real vocation- and indeed that of every Christian -is the vocation to contemplation.

Third, and most remarkable, this realization that she was indeed called to contemplation as a lay woman enabled her to stand on her own two feet and make her own decisions of conscience. Notice that the permission came not from Merton or from anybody else but from her own spirit. Contemplation brought her freedom and a sense of personal autonomy in making decisions in her life.

Finally, she knew that spiritually she could not stand still. She had to journey on- and the journey was toward a personal wholeness. (This is a good time to recall the introduction to this book that spoke of the conversion experiences we need to undergo)I would say that some of the convictions she arrived at through her experience of reading Merton are basic ingredients of a new way of thinking that has emerged in the Catholic Church and that has surfaced particularly in the latter half of the twentieth century. It has brought about a radical reshaping of American Catholic spirituality.

Devotional Spirituality

This notion of the laity as second class members was based on a spirituality that can be labeled "the spirituality of devotion." It was this spirituality that motivated not only lay persons; it could also be the spirituality of priests as well. In fact that's what I meant when I spoke earlier about my inability to pray and my failure to learn how to pray during my seminary years. The woman from the southwest, in the years before the Merton influence struck her, saw specific activities to express her relationship with God.

This spirituality of devotion was the spirituality that I also lived by before *my conversion*. So, I said prayers. I went to confession. I received communion. I prayed the rosary regularly. In doing these practices I was receiving grace. It was a *mediated* spirituality: by this I mean that I did not reach God directly but through the saying of prayers, by receiving the various sacraments. This spirituality simply assumed that any direct experience of God, as God is in Himself, belonged to a future that was beyond this life. It could not be a part of my religious experience in the present.

Dualism: This spirituality of devotion was more about doing than about being, more about behavior than about consciousness, more about pleasing God by carrying out God's commands rather than about experiencing God as God truly is. It was clearly a spirituality of *dualism* which stressed the transcendence of God as God's separateness from the world and from us. If divine condescension allows us to achieve some kind of communion with God, I must still speak of separateness when I speak of God.

Verbal: Devotional spirituality was strongly *verbal*. Words were very important: the words we used to speak of our relationship with God, the words we used to speak with God. Time honored phrases were preferred because heresy lurked beyond the corner of the careless phrase.

Speculative: This approach to spirituality tended almost inevitably to be quite *speculative*. It found its secure moorings in the doctrines of the church, in accepted dogmatic theology. Thinking correctly about God and using the right words were deep concerns. One must for example be precise and accurate in expressing the relationship between God and creation. While we see God as the cause of the world and also as the one who sustains it in existence and guides it by God's providence, still this approach is careful to avoid any words that might imply any identification of God with the world. Such identification might spell pantheism.

Contemplative Spirituality

While devotional spirituality tends to be a spirituality of doing, aimed at bettering our behavior to make us more pleasing to God, contemplative spirituality is best seen as a spirituality of being, aimed at deepening our consciousness and bringing us to an appreciation of our oneness with God and in God, of our oneness with one another and with all of creation in God.

The older spirituality was clearly dualistic, separating the sacred from the secular, the supernatural from the natural. It tended to overemphasize the transcendence of God and in doing so seemed to set God apart from creation. While accepting the omnipresence of God, the older spirituality was still inclined to present God as more present in some places than in others; to find the grace of God more available in some settings (the sacred) than in others (the secular). Contemplative spirituality, on the other hand, refuses to identify the transcendence of God with a vision of God guiding and sustaining the universe and the world of people from afar. *In contemplative spirituality God is the mystery that is at the heart of all reality.*

Contemplative spirituality is not primarily about prayer or methods of prayer. It is a spirituality that embraces the totality of our lives. Its first concern is with God. Ruthlessly it destroys the false gods, the idols we build and call god. It takes away from us the god of dualism in whom we had heretofore believed. It demands that we let go of a god who is patriarchal. At worst he -- and I use the word "he" advisedly to describe this god, for he is indeed male -- is the tyrant god who punishes us relentlessly when we are bad and doles out favors to us when we are good. At best, he is a god who is aloof from us. His abode is heaven and we are on earth where he watches us from afar He is there, and we are here. This god is a god easily recognizable to so many of us. For he is a god we have worshiped for a long time. Contemplative spirituality says we must give up this god, for he is not the true God.

Where Is God?

A person who wants to pray has to face the question: "Where do I find God?" or, put even simpler, "Where is God?" For those of us who belong to the pre-Vatican II period in the life of the Roman Catholic Church, the latter way of putting the question will surely send our memories scurrying back to that great museum piece of our past, the Baltimore Catechism; and out of memory's deep recesses will come the answer indelibly impressed there: "God is everywhere."

"God is everywhere!" I want to suggest that we pause a moment just to let the stupendous reality of that statement sink into our minds and hearts. Nothing can compare with such an impressive and moving statement. "God is everywhere!" Every time we say it or think about it, we should give ourselves some quiet time to recover from the full impact of this fantastic, fascinating truth. Every day sky writers should write it in the air above us. Countless blimps, like the one that hovers over Super-Bowls, should ride our skies regularly, trailing signs with the wondrous message: "God is everywhere". And it would be meet and just that this statement be placed on the first page of a 200 page-book, leaving the remaining 199 pages blank for people to reflect and recover from reading something so stupendous.

If you go back to the Baltimore Catechism, you will recall that, following this marvelous answer, the Catechism goes on to ask another question. Sadly, it's the wrong question. It asks: "If God is everywhere, why do we not see Him?" The answer given is :"We cannot see God, because God is a pure spirit and cannot be seen with bodily eyes." The reason I say that we have here the wrong question and answer is that they don't take us anywhere. We cannot see God, so the obvious reaction is "Let's get on to something else." It's a pity. Logically the next question should have been: "If God is everywhere, how can we experience God's presence?" Now there is a question that really goes somewhere. It is the question that is at the heart of any true spirituality. Answering it is the only way of giving meaning to the life of prayer. It is the way into contemplative prayer.

This magnificent statement: "God is everywhere" offers endless possibilities for fruitful reflection. Simply put, it means that, wherever we may be, we are in the presence of God. God is above us, below us, around us, outside of us, inside of us. When we drive our cars, we are in the presence of God. When we play golf or go to a ball game or read a good book or eat a meal or take a drink --we are in the presence of God. As we come together for a meal or a liturgy, we are in the presence of God. God is everywhere. There are no privileged places where God is more present than in others. For God is fully and totally present wherever God is. There may be places more conducive to prayer than others, like a Church building or the solitude of your room or a quiet walk in the woods. But this does not mean that God is more present in these places than in any other place. No, God is fully and totally everywhere.

Let me try to clarify this a bit more. Think of it in this way: you and I because of the wonderful advances in travel capabilities can be anywhere. Europe, China, Australia --you name it. So we can be anywhere, but we cannot be everywhere. We cannot be everywhere, because our very nature as creatures requires that we be somewhere. That is to say, we have to be in some particular place that has limits and boundaries to it. Thus if you take a trip to England, you can go anywhere in England, but, since you can only be in one place at a time, you always have to be somewhere. You can be in Oxford and then in Cambridge. But because Oxford and Cambridge are in different places, you can only be in one or the other. You cannot be in both at the same time. We always, I repeat, have to be somewhere, some place that has limits.

God, on the other hand is everywhere. Now, everywhere must not be thought of as a lot of "somewheres," as if you could say: "God sure is in a lot of places." No, "everywhere" transcends all "somewheres." There are no limits to God's presence. That is why, God must not be thought of as an Object. For an object --a building, a car, a woman, a man --is always somewhere, in some limited place. An object cannot be everywhere. Therefore, because God is everywhere, we must not think of God as an object. Most of the problems we have about God come from the mistake of thinking of God as an object -as a thing - as one thing alongside of a lot of other things.

An Important Difference

Even when we say that God is in some particular place (which we see as part of "everywhere") for instance, in the room where you are now, it is not the same as saying that a friend is sitting in a chair in the same room with you. It is true you can make the statement : "God is present in the room" and the further statement "My friend is present in the room." But it is in each case a very different kind of presence. You could be just as truly in that room if your friend were absent; or your friend could leave and you could say "goodbye" to her. Then you would no longer be in the presence of your friend, but you would be no less present in the room because she has departed it. But if God were to leave the room, we would be saying goodbye not just to God but to our very selves. For apart from God's presence, we simply do not exist. God is the necessary and indispensable setting of my very being.

WOW!

If God is everywhere, that means that we are at all times **in the situation, the setting, that makes prayer possible.** For we are at all times in the presence of the One whom we desire to touch, to reach, in prayer. We don't have to go looking for God, as if God were somehow missing from our lives. An amusing story illustrates this. One day two young boys were walking down the street and passed a church. One of them said to the other: "Jeez, Mike, I ain't been to confession in a long time. I think I'll go now." They entered the church. Joey went into the confessional. "I want to go to confession, Father," he said. The priest told him to begin his confession. It had been a long time. The lad mumbled: "I don't know how to do it." The confessor, deciding this boy needed some instruction, began testing his knowledge of the catechism. He asked: "Where is God?" The lad, bewildered, said: "Beg your pardon, Father?" The priest repeated his question more emphatically: "Where is God?" Thereupon the young boy jumped up, ran out of the confessional, grabbed his friend by the hand, rushing him out of the Church: "Mike," he said in a trembling voice, "we gotta get out of here. God's missing and they think we've got him."

Okay it's a bit corny, but God isn't missing. We don't have to search for God. We don't have to find God. It is not that God is **there** and we are **here.** Rather God is there and here and everywhere. We are, as I say, **always in the setting or situation of prayer.** We might express it this way: God **is** always in touch with us, because we are always in God's saving presence. But we are not always in touch with God, because so often we are forgetful of the Presence of God.

God Is the Ground and Source of All

Being in the presence of God is not only the setting in which we work and pray, it is the necessary condition of our existence and of the existence of everything that is. When we say God is everywhere, we don't mean that God is *just there* in a static sort of way. No, God is, if I may put it this way, effortlessly busy everywhere. God is the *Source* of my being and the *Ground* of Love which enables me to continue in being. And this is true of everyone and everything that exists. Being in the presence of God is not something I choose, as if I were to say: "I guess I'll spend some time in the presence of God today." Or, "I'm going on retreat next week. I'll be able to spend a lot of time in the presence of God." No, being in God's presence is not a matter of choice. It is not, for example, like saying: "I think I will go visit my friend in the hospital." Being in the presence of God is an ontological necessity. The salesman for American

Express Cheques used to say: "Don't go anywhere without them." But we can, if we so choose. But we can't go anywhere without God. For "anywhere without God" is simply the realm of non-existence. It is quite literally nowhere.

Who Is God?

The hymn "How Great Thou Art," which Roman Catholics at one time would have disdainfully dismissed as "Protestant," has in recent years become very popular in Catholic worship. Some weeks ago a priest friend of mine told me of a non-liturgical setting he has discovered for that hymn: every morning, as he shaves and sees himself in the mirror, the words come spontaneously to his lips: "How great thou art." Whatever you might want to say about my friend's need to cultivate a bit more humility, it is important to understand that his extra-liturgical use of this song has drastically changed the meaning of the word "great." No one, including my boastful friend, is great as God is great. The word "great" applied to God takes on a radically different meaning from that same word applied to humans. Thus, it would be true to say that God is "great," because something of what we consider "great" in humans is in God; at the same time it would be equally true to say that God is "not great," because the puny greatness of creatures is as nothing compared to the greatness of God. It isn't simply that God has a lot more greatness than we could possibly have; rather God's greatness completely transcends whatever we might call greatness in any human person.

A word from Meister Eckhart, the fourteenth century Rhenish mystic. With that lucid ambiguity so characteristic of him, says: "The Divine One is a negation of negations and a denial of denials." He goes on to clarify: Every creature contains a negative, namely, a denial that it is the other.

God contains the denial of denials. God is the One who denies of every other that it is anything except Himself."

If his meaning seems to be eluding you, let me try to clarify his "clarification." What he is saying is that every creature is finite, which is to say that it is limited in what it is. A particular creature is only "this;" it is not "that." It is their limited being that distinguishes one creature from another. To say that a house is a house is to deny that it is a horse. This is what Eckhart means when he tells us that every creature contains a negative: a denial that it is the other.

After telling his congregation (these words, I should point out, are from one of his sermons! How would you like to belong to his congregation!) that every creature is a denial that it is anything other than itself, he goes on to speak about God and says that God is a denial of denials. First God is a denial that He is "this" or "that." Now "this" or "that" represents each and every created reality: a house, a horse, a tree, a flower, a woman, a man, etc., etc. This seems clear enough: because God is God, because God transcends all created reality, God is a denial that He is any thing that we experience in the created world.

God is not to be located among creatures. We can imagine lining up all created objects, things, persons. God could not be one of them, for God transcends all created beings. But Eckhart says more (and now things get really complicated!): God is a denial of denials. In other words, God is a denial that He is *not* "this;" God is a denial that He is *not* "that." God is a denial that He is *not* any and every creature that exists. Does this sound pretty heavy? Try thinking of it in this way. Eckhart is saying that, while God is not "this" or "that", **there is yet a sense in which God is "this" and "that," and indeed that**

God is every creature that exists -- not in any pantheistic way, but in the sense that, apart from God, neither "this" nor "that" nor any creature could exist. Why? Because God is the Source and Ground of each and every creature that is. Every "this," every "that," every creature, exists only because it finds its being, identity and uniqueness in God. Apart from God, it simply could not be.[A tip: *Eckhart is saying there are two negatives in God. The first (stating that God is not "this" or "that") affirms the divine transcendence. The second (stating in a negative way the positive truth that God is the Ground of all that exists) affirms the divine immanence.*] Okay, that's enough of Eckhart.

God As Mystery

The God of contemplative spirituality is a God of mystery. God is the unknown and the unknowable. The ancient description of the Tao can be applied to talk about God "The one who speaks does not know; the one who knows does not speak." The one who speaks doesn't know, because the reality of God cannot be expressed in human language -- the best we can do is use metaphors. As Meister Eckhart (woops here he is again) put it in his inimitable blunt way: "One who speaks about God lies." At the same time, the one who knows does not speak, for the reality of God is too huge a burden for human language to bear. The best speech about the ineffable God therefore, is silence.

Talking about prayer, Merton writes: "To pray is to enter into a mystery. When we do not enter into the unknown we do not pray." He also says that a real inner life and a life of true freedom begin when we enter into communion with the unknown with in us. This, he goes on to say, makes it possible for us to enter into communion with the same unknown in others.

To the Students at Smith College

In 1967 writing to the students at Smith College and commenting on their reading and sharing of his writings, Merton speaks of his oneness with them and says there is no greater happiness than *the happiness of being at one with everything in that hidden ground of love* for which there can be no explanations. In a letter written about a year later -- to a Dr. Weis Kopf – Merton once again speaks of the ground of being. Here is what he says. I summarize his statement : The ultimate ground in which all contradictions are united and all comes out right is, for the Christian, personal, that is to say, a ground of freedom and love.

To the Novices at Gethsemani

Speaking to the novices at Gethsemani, Merton speaks clearly and beautifully the mystery about prayer and the mystery of God. He writes: "Prayer is not only the lifting up of the mind and heart to God but it is also the response to God within us. It ultimately leads to the discovery and fulfillment of our own true self in God. We should not therefore, regard prayer as if we are clients seeking an answer from God… He seeks us more than we seek him. If we love him, he has first loved us. But let us recognize, too, that we do not know ourselves and we know him so us. We do not understand their own needs and desires; how can we understand his desires in our regard? Prayer that is always shrouded in mystery. To pray is to enter into mystery. When we do not enter into the unknown, we do not pray. If we want everything in our prayer life to be abundantly clear at all times it will by that very fact defeat our prayer life. Prayer is an expression of our complete dependence on a hidden and mysterious God. It is therefore nourished by humility and a sense of indigence, and by compunction.""

We should never seek to reach some supposedly summit of prayer out of spiritual ambition, for this would be a sure way to frustrate his own intentions. We should not seek to enter deeply into the life of prayer in order to glory in it as an achievement however spiritual, but because in this way we can come close to the Lord... who seeks to give us a strong dose of his love."

A Friend

There is a person to whom I have been giving spiritual direction for some time. Gradually I have encouraged her to do less thinking and less discursive reasoning in her private prayer and to spend more time in wordless prayer. On one occasion she said to me: "I used to think of prayer as friendly conversation with God. I imagined God at my side and myself speaking with God as I would with a friend. Now, while I know that that is a legitimate metaphor for prayer and there are times when I still find it useful, more and more in my private prayer, I feel the need of going beyond images and words. Strangely, as I have let myself be drawn more and more in this direction, I have found that God has become more and more a mystery to me. Yet unaccountably I feel there is more depth in my prayer. I really experience that I am touching God or, perhaps better, that I am being touched by God."

Thomas Merton in a talk to the novices at Gethsemani, given in Lent of 1961, said: "To pray is to enter into mystery, and when we do not enter into the unknown, we do not pray. If we want everything in our prayer-life to be abundantly clear at all times, we will by that very fact defeat our prayer-life." In a letter, written in 1966 to John Hunt, who was then senior editor of the Saturday Evening Post, Merton said much the same thing: "A true inner life of freedom (surely one way of viewing prayer) begins when we enter into communion with the unknown within us." Then he adds a further observation, namely, that such communion with the unknown in ourselves makes it possible for us "to enter into communion with the same unknown in others."

Are You Disappointed?

At this point, dear reader, you may be disappointed that I started out to answer for you the question "who is God?" and I seem to be suggesting that there really isn't any answer. Maybe the reason for your reaction, if that has been your reaction, is that you think of mystery as something that must be solved. But I would want to say that calling God mystery amounts to extending an invitation to probe ever more deeply into the reality of God, though with the realization that one will never be able to exhaust the meaningfulness of God. To call God mystery is to remind ourselves that all the knowledge we have of God comes from some human experience of God. The words we possess are able to express only the human experience, not the divine reality experienced. ***That is why all the language we use about God is metaphorical.*** When we speak about God we are always using analogies. We have no divine language, only human.

Think of the many names of God that we find in the Bible: our Savior, our Redeemer and Deliverer, our Refuge, our Helper, our Shepherd, our Ruler, our Mother, our Father, our Lover, etc. If we reflect on them, we note that they are all *relational:* we relate to God as the One who is our Source and

Sustainer, the One who cares for us and provides for us. *This is to say that we are talking about a God who loves us.*

God Is Love

When the scriptures say that "God is Love," they are drawing on a human experience: all of us, hopefully, love and are loved. Now love is the deepest of all human mysteries. We can experience it, but we cannot adequately explain what it is we are experiencing. Hence, when we say "God is Love," we are not resolving the mystery of God; rather we are touching the mystery of God with another mystery. Love is as incomprehensible as God. Still we have experiences of love in our lives and these experiences can help us to understand a little more clearly who God is.

In one of his reading notebooks, Merton quotes a saying of Allah attributed to the prophet Mohammed: "My earth and heaven cannot contain me, but the heart of my believing servant contains me." Merton comments: "The heart only is capable of knowing God." The heart is the only place strong enough to bear the divine secret; and the divine secret is that the Ground of being, which sustains all that is, is the Hidden Ground of Love. To know God as the Hidden Ground of Love is to know that we are loved.

In *Contemplative Prayer*, Merton writes: "Our knowledge of God is paradoxically a knowledge not of Him as the object of our scrutiny, but of ourselves as utterly dependent on His saving and merciful knowledge of us." In a letter to Etta Gullick, a friend in England who confided to him her desire to love God more than everything that exists, Merton readily identifies with this desire; yet he adds: "Beyond all is a love of God in and through all that exists. We must not hold them apart one from another. But he must be One in all, and Is.

"So, my friends, let us sing "How Great Thou Art," preferably in liturgy rather than into a shaving mirror. But remember that no words or images of ours can ever probe the meaning of God's greatness. Only love can know. Or in Pascal's words: "The heart has its reasons which reason does not know."

Awareness of God's Presence

Consider the following parable. A wife and husband are sitting in their living room. She is knitting; he is devouring the sports' page of the paper. All at once she says to him with quiet sarcasm: "You can stop saying: 'Yes, dear,' every five minutes. I stopped talking to you a half hour ago." The parable describes a breakdown of communication and probably an unhealthy relationship: a husband talking perfunctorily to his wife, yet not really aware of her presence. Suppose we read the parable in the light of our relationship with God. We are always in the presence of God. Yet we can pray to God in a distracted, perfunctory way, without really being aware of God's presence. Now the husband in our parable could go on saying "Yes, dear," even after his wife had gotten up and left the room. Nothing much would change except that she wouldn't be there. The situation would be quite different with us, if we were talking to God and all at once God decided to leave. Since the presence of God is the necessary condition of our very existence, we could not, if God were to leave us, go on mechanically saying our prayers. For if God removed the divine presence from us, we would simply cease to be.

Always in the Presence of God

We cannot be without the presence of God. But we can be without being aware of God's presence. Yet to live without awareness of God is to live in a world of illusion. It is to be out of touch with the real world. **The Great Fact** of our lives is that we are always in the presence of God. **The Great Problem** of our lives is that we are so often unaware of God's presence. We can go for days without ever adverting to that presence. We can be unaware of God's Presence, even when we pray, as for instance when we pray and our awareness is on a hundred other things. We can also be unaware of God in prayer, if we pray to a God who is distant from us, as if we were here and God there. No, God is closer to us than our inmost self. In fact, there is a sense in which God is my inmost self; or, if that way of putting it might seem to border on the unorthodox, let me say it this way: when I find my deepest self, I shall discover God, because God is the Ground of Love in which I exist.

What Will Heaven Mean?

Let me make this very concrete by saying: *Each of us, right now, at this very moment is as fully in the presence of God as we shall ever be.* Even in heaven we shall not be any more fully in the presence of God than we are at this moment. The enormous difference heaven will make is that in heaven we shall be *fully and always* **aware** that we are in the presence of God. This calls for a rethinking of our notion of heaven. Too often we picture heaven as a kind of Hawaiian InterContinental Hotel which initially is empty and then gradually fills up, as guests arrive who have the proper reservations. Actually, heaven isn't a place we go to. Rather it is Someone we go to. That is what heaven really is. It is, quite simply, becoming ourselves fully and totally. This will happen, not when

God becomes more fully present to us, but when we are *always fully aware that we are in God's presence.*

If you reflect on this for half a second, you will realize the amazing truth that all along we have been in paradise. But we don't know it. If we were fully aware, we would know that we are in paradise. For paradise, heaven, is simply God's Presence possessed in full and total attentiveness.

Original Sin

One way of understanding that mystery that we call **original sin** is to see it as a forgetfulness of the presence of God. In the Genesis myth of paradise the man and the woman are fully aware of God's presence. The fall is not a fall into the real world, but into a world of illusion, in which they failed to see what is most important to all reality, namely, the presence of God. One way of understanding Jesus' redemption is that he awakens us from the long sleep of forgetfulness and by his grace we are once again able to be aware of God.

What Original Sin Means

To put this another way: we no longer see things as they truly are. Where there is oneness, we see separateness. Where there is harmony, we see alienation and manipulation of people. Is not so much that this oneness is taken away. It is present in us, hidden in the depths of our being, but it lies there forgotten.

I have described heaven as full awareness of God's presence, being alive to the holy presence. If you look at Thomas Merton's description of contemplation in the very first chapter of *New Seeds of Contemplation,* you will discover that that is precisely the way in which he defines contemplation.

Contemplation is the highest expression of man's intellectual and spiritual life. It is that life itself, fully active, fully aware that it is alive...It is a vivid realization of the fact that life and being in us proceed from an invisible, transcendent and infinitely abundant Source. **Contemplation is, above all, awareness of that Source...Contemplation is a sudden gift of awareness,** an awakening to the Real in all that is real. A vivid awareness of our contingent reality as received, as a present from God, as a free gift of love.

Is contemplation, then, a bit like the Emerald Isle, "a little bit of heaven"? Almost, but not quite. For this side of the eschatological divide, we experience the presence of God by faith, not by a face to face vision. Also the experience of God in contemplation is a free gift of God that comes when God chooses to give it. Hence it is not a constant in our lives. Still it is the closest we can come to heaven in this life. It is the moment when we are fully alive, fully awakened to the Real in all that is real and, therefore, fully in love with all that is.

Degrees of Awareness

I wrote a book on prayer some time ago, called *Seeking the Face of God.* In it I identified contemplative prayer as awareness of God. I wrote a second book on prayer, *Silence on Fire,* to clarify more precisely what I meant by the "prayer of awareness." What I was really doing in this second book was hinting that I had made a mistake, in the earlier book, by identifying contemplation and the "prayer of awareness." For the term "awareness of the presence of God" can admit of degrees. It can mean all those levels of awareness which, however deep they may be, fall short of that total awareness of God which alone deserves the name of contemplation. Contemplation is always a gift of God, which comes when God offers it. We cannot achieve it by ourselves. What

I want to call "prayer of awareness" is any level of wordless prayer which opens our hearts to God's presence, apprehended by faith, and prepares us for that total awareness that is contemplation. Yet I wouldn't want to draw too sharp a distinction between the two, for "prayer of awareness" is often on the very borders of contemplation and not infrequently invades its very territory.

Contemplation and Consciousness

One way of understanding contemplation is to think of it in terms of consciousness. Chuang Tzu, the Taoist philosopher, whom Merton was fond of says *that he had a dream. "I, Chuang Tzu,* dreamed I was a butterfly fluttering hither and thither to all intents and purposes a butterfly... suddenly I awakened... Now I do not know whether I was then a man dreaming I was a butterfly or whether I am now a butterfly dreaming that I am a man." Chuang Tzu's reflection on his experience is not as odd as at first hearing it might seem to be. The question he is posing is an important one, namely, what is the state of consciousness that puts us in touch with what is truly real? We all recognize the difference between dream consciousness and ordinary waking consciousness.

An Example

Let me suppose that I had a dream last night, and in the dream I was standing on the edge of a very high cliff, looking down at huge jagged rocks below. Suddenly, to my horror, the ground gives way beneath me and I feel myself falling toward the jagged rocks.

In the middle of the fall I wake from my dream, perhaps with a cry of terror. As I arrived at ordinary waking consciousness, I experienced a deep sense of relief, when I realize that what seemed to be happening to me was not happening after all. It was only a dream. I had not been falling. There was no cliff. There were no jagged rocks.

What has happened to change fear into peaceful relief? It's that I have moved from one state of consciousness to another. While I was in the dream state the dream objects were very real to me. It was only when I awakened that I realized that the dream objects had no substance. When I pass from the dream state to the state of ordinary waking consciousness I repudiated the dream objects.

Suppose however, that I were to enter into a dream state and never wake up from the dream I would continue to experience the dream objects as if they were real. I would never repudiate them. For, in order to do so it would be necessary for me to move to another level of consciousness namely the state of ordinary waking consciousness.

A Still Higher State of Consciousness

But let us think of yet a further possibility: suppose that the state of being awake at the state of ordinary waking consciousness is not the state of a *truly awakened consciousness* after all. Suppose there is a level of consciousness beyond our ordinary state of being awake, which, if you were to enter it, would give you a completely new and exciting experience. This new experience would enable you to see that the objects of ordinary waking consciousness, which for so long a time you took to be real, are actually as illusory as the objects of the dream. Once you awakened to this new state of heightened consciousness you would repudiate the objects of ordinary waking consciousness. In repudiating them you would at last be fully awake, fully in touch with what is truly real. You would have recovered your original face. You would have been fully reborn into the life of God. You would have returned to paradise.

A Spiritual Revolution

The experience of contemplation, therefore, goes far beyond a change in behavior. It is nothing less than a spiritual revolution that awakens deep levels of consciousness in us, not just the surface consciousness of our superficial selves but the inner depths consciousness of our real self which we experience as nothing apart from the being of God. It is the experience of utter joy. Merton writes: "The only true joy on earth is to escape from the prison of our own false self and enter by love into union with the life who dwells and sings within the essence of every creature in the core of our own souls."

An Invitation

I would like to invite you to a daily practice of the "prayer of awareness." It doesn't require anything special. It simply means spending time just being in the presence of God in silence and wordlessness, though one need not be too much of a purist: we may need an occasional word to help preserve our attentiveness. One happy thing about this approach to prayer: you don't have to get anywhere. For you are already and always there: in the presence of God. You are just wanting to be more attentive and more lovingly responsive to that presence. "Not getting anywhere" may seem discouraging and could tempt one to give up the practice of "prayer of awareness." But I guarantee that such prayer, daily adhered to, will do things to us. It will make us more loving, more considerate, more compassionate toward our sisters and brothers. For sooner or later our awareness of God's presence leads us to awareness of God's people.

Thinking or Awareness

One warning I need to issue. Do not confuse "awareness" of God with "thinking" about God. Fr. Emile LaSalle, who teaches spirituality at Sophia University in Tokyo says: "One of my most difficult tasks is to teach people not to think."

Let me offer a simple example of the difference between "thinking" and "being aware." Several years ago, I was at the National Gallery in London. At the time they had a special display of Leonardo da Vinci's marvelous drawing (unfinished) of "The Virgin and Child with St. Elizabeth and St. John the Baptist." It was in a small room all by itself, with a bench in the center of the room where one could sit quietly and look. For about half an hour I sat there, all alone, powerfully moved by this masterpiece. Now during that time, I could have thought about that drawing and analyzed what made it a masterpiece. I could have noted the peculiar darkness in Elizabeth's eyes and compared that to the light in Mary's. I could have looked at the child of St. Elizabeth and noted how his eyes were fixed on Jesus. I could have looked into the face of Jesus and seen the pensive, reflective look on his face. I would, in doing all these things, be thinking about the drawing. Notice how the thinking separates me from the drawing. I am a subject analyzing an object. The more I think of it the more distance I place between it and myself. But suppose that, instead of thinking about it, I simply sat there in awe, allowing myself to be drawn into the beauty before me. Totally forgetful of myself,

I could let the drawing's beauty become so identified with me that I would become one with the drawing. I would no longer be a subject analyzing an object. I as a separate subject would just disappear. I would be so absorbed that the drawing and I would have become one.

Thinking is an experience that divides. Awareness is an experience that unifies. Prayer of awareness unites us with God. We disappear, as it were, and our subjectivity becomes one with the subjectivity of God.

Two More Examples

Because it is so very important I want to insist once again that we understand this difference between thinking and awareness. So let me give you a couple other examples.

Suppose you see a beautiful red rose. You can think about that rose if you choose. That means that you as a subject examined the rose and its characteristics as an object. You notice it has a green stem, some leaves, and lovely red petals; you can count the number of petals. You can go further and examine the rose in a laboratory. Notice how you are putting distance between yourself and the rose. You are a subject analyzing the rose as an object but suppose that, instead of thinking about the rose in this discursive way, you simply look at it and let yourself be drawn into the beauty of color, the fragrance, the comeliness of shape. The more you look at it and let yourself become absorbed in it, the more you forget about yourself. There is no longer subject viewing an object. You become one with the rose in the sense that you as a separate subject are no longer there.

Here is another example. Think of a professional singer making plans for a concert performance. There is a big difference between what she does in preparation for the concert and what she does at the actual performance. In her preparation she will have to do a good bit of thinking: about the music and its notation, about her voice and the way she would use it, about the text and the emotions it evokes, and probably about a lot of things I don't even know. There is a subject, the singer and an object, the music. And the two are separate. She may also do some talking with her singing coach. She may even say a prayer or two. But all this takes place before the performance. As the performance approaches the distance between subject and object lessens. Finally when the performance takes place, the singer, if she is a good artist, will not be thinking of any of these things (the music, her voice, her feelings.) She will quite literally become lost in her singing. It will not then be a case of a singer plus a performance. In a sense she will no longer be there: she will be one with the music. There will be pure Song. In the words of T. S. Eliott: "the music heard so deeply/that is not heard at all, but you are the music/while the music lasts."

Back to the Prayer of Awareness

In a somewhat similar way, there will be times in our lives when we will think about God, in reading, and study, and in prayer with words. These are necessary elements of a true spirituality. But the time comes when you will want to pass beyond the old and give ourselves to prayer without words or ideas or images, to wordless prayer. This prayer of pure awareness, in which there is neither subject nor object is what Thomas Merton means by contemplation. Writing in *New Seeds of Contemplation*, he says: "In the depths of contemplative prayer there seems to be no division between subject and object and there is no reason to make any statements about God or about oneself. He is and this reality absorbs everything else."

The Importance of This Kind of Prayers

It is this kind of prayer above all, I believe, that gives meaning and inner depths to our lives. It is so easy to live our lives simply on the surface. A routine of life that is subject to things and almost wholly taken up with what is outside ourselves is bound to be a life of illusion and lack of freedom. We become people who are always looking out, never looking in. We never catch even fleeting glimpses of what is truly real. Speaking of a different kind of life -- one which is in touch with its own inner reality, Merton writes:

> "The real inner life and freedom of man begins when this inner dimension opens up and man lives in communion with the unknown within himself. On the basis of this he can also be in communion with the same unknown in others."

It is awareness that enables us to find the unknown in ourselves and in others. We experience God's presence everywhere. The world which was once opaque to us becomes translucent and we know at last, because we have experienced it, the truth of that wondrous statement in the old Baltimore Catechism, God is everywhere.

> How nice
>
> To be
>
> Aware
>
> That God
>
> Is here
>
> And there
>
> And everywhere

Finding Our Identity in God

Some time ago a young couple who are friends of mine decided they would go on sabbatical for a year in southwest, USA. Sally was a writer and Jim a school teacher. They had been able to save enough money to make the sabbatical possible and were looking forward to it with joy. Sally told me that during the sabbatical she hoped to engage in some reflection, some praying and, because she is a writer, to try to finish a book she had been working on for some time.

Two or three months went by. One day I received a rather despondent letter from Sally, saying that she seemed to be getting nowhere in her writing and was quite discouraged about it. I wrote reminding her that she had gone on this sabbatical to have time for rest, reflection and praying. I said, further, that I thought she should not let herself get caught up in the production-oriented mentality of our society and think that her sabbatical would be a failure if she did not "produce something." I suggested to her that it was enough for her simply to "be" during her sabbatical. There really wasn't anything she <u>had</u> to do.

She wrote back and thanked me for sharing my reflections and said: "Now when people ask me what I do, I simply tell that I am a human being."

Being and Doing

We all have to learn that we must be, each of us, a human being before we are a human doing. We have to discover ever more deeply the value of silence and quiet and solitude. We need to get over the fear we sometimes have that "we are doing nothing" or that we have "nothing to do." Isn't it odd that so many of us are quite accomplished in wasting time, but aren't at all good at "doing nothing" And by that I mean "doing nothing and just being." It is only in being (which calls for some kind of quiet and a relaxed atmosphere) that we can come to know who we are. If we are only "do-ers," and never "be-ers," we shall never really know who it is that is doing what we do. We shall be strangers to ourselves. And strangers to God too; for our being is the "place" of our union with God.

Unfortunately our culture does not encourage us to find joy and contentment in times when we are able just to be. Thomas Merton more than once reminded his readers that in a culture which makes us believe that every minute has to be put to some useful purpose, we have to learn the value of the useless. Read his sparkling essay, "Rain and the Rhinoceros," in *Raids on the Unspeakable.* Here is a brief, teasing sampling:

"One who is not alone has not discovered his identity. He seems to be alone, perhaps, for he experiences himself as 'individual.' But because he is willingly enclosed and limited by the laws and illusions of collective existence, he has no more identity than an unborn child in the womb. He is not yet conscious. He is alien to his own truth. He has life, but no identity. To have an identity he has to be awake and aware...of the invulnerable inner reality which we cannot recognize (which we can only be), but to which we awaken only when we see the unreality of our vulnerable shell. The discovery of this inner self is an act and affirmation of solitude." (pp. 14-15)

Letting Go

That "invulnerable inner reality," that "inner self" is our identity. To discover it we have need of some solitude, in which we can become experts at doing nothing and just being. This calls for a good bit of letting go. We must, at some times in our lives, let go of the things that are in our minds and hearts: our thoughts, our plans, our desires, our concerns, our anxieties. Putting them aside for a time does not mean that we do not have to deal with them at the proper time. But there must be some moments in our lives when, for the while at least, we let go of them (so that later we can deal with them afresh).

This "letting go" is difficult. For our minds are going all the time --like a watch I used to have that was kept going simply by the motion of the hand without ever having to be wound up. We don't have to be wound up either: we are so deluged with thoughts, feelings, concerns that we are scarcely aware of their diversity, or sometimes even of their presence. They fragment us and scatter our energies. They hide our inner unity. They prevent us, therefore, from knowing who we are.

Yet fearfully we hang on to our activities, because somehow or other we feel that letting go of them poses a threat to our very identity. Descartes' dictum "Cogito, ergo sum" ("I think, therefore I am") gets translated into "Ago, ergo sum" ("I act, therefore I am"). This is to say that I am sure that I am, precisely because I do something, whether that something be thinking or some other type of activity. So we tend to look upon our walking, talking, seeing, speaking, thinking as if they constituted our personal identity. Apart from them, we seem scarcely to exist.

We need to learn that just being, without doing anything, is a fruitful, even necessary, form of prayer. It is at the heart of the "prayer of awareness." Thomas Merton wrote to Sr. Therese Lentfoehr who had asked him about prayer:

> "About prayer: have you a garden or somewhere that you can walk in, by yourself? Take half an hour or fifteen minutes a day and just walk up and down among the flowerbeds...Do not try to think about anything in particular and when thoughts about work, etc. come to you, do not try to push them out by main force, but see if you can drop them just by relaxing your mind. Do this because you are "praying...But if thoughts about work will not go away, accept them idly and without too much eagerness, with the intention of letting God reveal His will to you through these thoughts."(RJ, 195)

A Warning

Spending time "just being" does not allow us by any means to shun the responsibilities that are ours: the things that we must do to live our own lives fully and to be attentive to the needs of our sisters and brothers. But the time of letting go in prayer will help us to keep things in balance so that our daily activities do not overwhelm us and fragment our inner unity. Time spent in "just being" will give us a new sense of who we are. It will strengthen us to do better whatever it is we have to do. For we will really be there in the doing. Once we have discovered our identity in God, we will have more accurate insight into life and the priorities we need to set for ourselves. We may come to learn that many of the things that once unsettled us, we are now able to take in stride.

The Tiger and the Sheep

There is an oft-told Hindu story about the tiger and the sheep. Once upon a time there was a flock of sheep grazing peacefully in the fields. A female tiger chanced upon them. She happened to be pregnant, but still her tiger instincts moved her to attack the sheep. In the course of her leap, she gave birth to a baby tiger, but died in the process. The sheep, seeing the dead tiger, finally had the courage to return. They discovered the baby tiger and, pitying this poor orphan, adopted him. The "teachers" in the flock taught him how to bleat and how to chew grass. He was a slow learner, but eventually mastered it and discovered what he thought was his identity, namely, being a sheep.

One day the sheep were in a field again, grazing. Along came another tiger. He attacked the sheep and they all scurried away --all that is, but the little tiger. He just stood there almost casually. He wasn't afraid at all. In fact he looked up at the big tiger and bleated at him. The big tiger was disgusted with such conduct. He grabbed the little tiger by the ear and took him to a pool of water and had him look in and see that he was the image and likeness of the big tiger. But the little tiger didn't get it. So the big tiger took him to his cave, where he had the remains of a deer he had killed the day before. He tried to get the little tiger to eat some of the flesh, but the little fellow turned away, nauseated by the sight. Finally, in desperation the big one opened the mouth of the little one and forced some of the meat into his mouth. The little tiger tasted the blood running down his throat and began to chew. Then suddenly everything was changed---and he let out the roar of a tiger! All his life he had mistaken his identity: his "culture" made him think he was a sheep. He never took the time out to discover who he really was. Now in this moment in the cave he discovered at last that he was not a sheep, but a tiger. He found his true identity.

The prayer of awareness, wordless prayer, the prayer of "just being," is our going into the cave to discover and rediscover ever more fully our true identity. Unless we find regular times in our lives simply to be, our "doing" will chop us to bits. It will so compartmentalize our lives that we may never come to know who we are. We will live our lives as bleating tigers eating grass.

Finding Our Brothers and Sisters in God

In December 1966 John Hunt, senior editor of *The Saturday Evening Post* wrote to Thomas Merton inviting him to write an article on monasticism for that journal's "Speaking Out" column. Merton was interested, but had his own ideas about what he should say to the readers of *The Post*. He proposed an article with the title "Speaking Out For the Inside." The point of the article would be to help people realize that life does have an interior dimension of depth and awareness. The unfortunate predicament of so many people is that this interiority is blocked out by a life that concentrates on externals.

The plight of these people (this is Shannon speaking, not Merton) might be likened to that of the people of Europe before the discovery of the New World. The only world they knew was Europe; and all the while there was a whole other world, full of new and marvelous things of which they knew nothing. That world was there, but they were unaware. Once they discovered it, all sorts of new adventures became possible.

In a somewhat similar way people who know only the externals of life are cut off from a realm of their own reality that offers new and exciting experiences that far surpass the kind of life that is possible at the level of just the superficial.

A Clarification

In the course of clarifying to John Hunt what he would write about in the *Saturday Evening Post* (I am back to Merton again, though I should say that the article he intended was never actually written), Merton says: "The inner life and freedom of man begins when this inner dimension opens up and man lives *in communion with the unknown within himself.* On the basis of this, he can also be *in communion with the same unknown in others.*"

Perceptive readers may recall that I made reference to this text earlier, though without lingering on it. Now is the time for lingering. In his writings on spirituality Merton is constantly pointing to the existence of this marvelous interior life in all of us. When we miss it, we miss most of what is truly real in us.

To speak of this divine presence in us is simply to particularize the general theme running through all this chapter, namely, "that God is everywhere." Yet it is only when we begin to experience God in the depths of our own being that this wondrous truth "God is everywhere" ceases to be merely an article of faith we believe in or a conclusion of reason we assent to and becomes a reality of personal experience. It becomes what Merton calls a "communion with the Unknown" within us.

The Unkown in Us and in All Else

But this is only a beginning. Our inner life does not exist in isolation. It is linked with the inner life of everyone else. How can I say this? Because the "Unknown" whom we meet in our depths is the same "Unknown" who dwells in the depths of all of God's people. This is why Merton can say "communion with the Unknown" in ourselves becomes the basis for "communion with that same Unknown in others." *I wish there were some way I could make these words leap off the page and really grab you. They are aweinspiring!* What they say to me is that in experiencing God in the depths of my being, I also experience each and every one of you, because you also are in communion with God. In God we are truly one with one another. I am one with each and everyone of you and all of you with me.

An Example

Let me make this very concrete. Suppose you are at a shopping mall. You watch people milling about, going in and out of a various stores. As you see them on the surface of reality, they seem to be all separate from one another. Yet if you move to a deeper level on consciousness, --that level wherein alone you see reality as it really is. The level wherein alone you meet the "Unknown" in yourselves as the same "Unknown" who is in these "others," you are able to let go of the "illusion" of separateness. You are able to see that you and they are all one.

Merton and Louisville

It was rather sneaky of me to write the above paragraph. For I was really describing an actual experience that Thomas Merton had. On March 18, 1958, he had gone into Louisville to see about the printing of a new postulants' guidebook. Standing at the corner of Fourth and Walnut Streets, he had a deep experience of interiority. He saw people going in and coming out of stores in a shopping district (there weren't any malls then). All at once he was overwhelmed with the realization that he loved these people and that they belonged to him as he belonged to them. He was snapped forever out of the illusion of thinking that because he lived in a monastery and followed an ancient rule that he was somehow separate from them. He was energized by the joy of simply being a human person and united with, not separated from, the rest of the human race.

Later as he reflected on the experience and wrote about it, he was moved by the splendor of it all: "Then it was as if I suddenly saw the secret beauty of their hearts, the depths of their hearts, where neither sin nor desire nor self-knowledge can reach, the core of their being, the person that each one is in God's eyes. If only they could see themselves as they really *are*. If only we could see each other that way all the time. There would be no more war, no more hatred, no more greed." *(Conjectures of a Guilty Bystander,* 158)

Awakening to a New Sense of Responsibility

This experience awakened in Merton a sense of responsibility to his fellow men and women and moved him to involvement, through his writings, in the great social issues of his day. So too for us: as soon as we let go of the notion of separateness, we know that we are responsible for one another, especially for those who are in need. My responsibilities to the homeless, the sick, the needy, the oppressed, the marginalized spring from that deep oneness in God that I have with them and with all my sisters and brothers. I must love them as myself, for in a very real way they are "my other self." As Thomas Merton said at Calcutta in a gathering of people from many religious traditions: "We are already one. But we imagine that we are not. And what we have to recover is our original unity. What we have to be is what we are." *(Asian Journal, 308)*

The equation of Christian social responsibility is this: coming to know God in our own inner selves means coming to know people and coming to know people means getting involved with them and with their problems. And that involvement takes place in history, in the here-and-now of their lifetime and ours. Thomas Merton in a 1966 article in *Commonweal* articulates a "ministry" insight that grew out of his contemplative experience: "That I should have been born in 1915, that I should be the contemporary of Auschwitz, Hiroshima and the Watts riots are things about which I was not first consulted. Yet they are also events in which, whether I like it or not, *I* am *deeply and personally involved."*

What of Ourselves?

If we have really become aware of our oneness with all our sisters and brothers, dare we be uninvolved in the predicaments that belong to their history and ours? In our day which has witnessed so many wars a particular area of responsibility for us is to work for peace. This means, I believe that we are called to a commitment of non-violence. For non-violence is simply the other side of contemplation.

Later in this chapter I will talk briefly of this link between contemplation and non-violence.

Without doubt it can be said that the most serious area of responsibility we have toward our sisters and brothers is to rid our world of war and all the threats to peace. For Merton, and also for me, this especially means a commitment to non-violence. I want to speak of this in a little more detail later in this chapter.

A Moving Story

I read recently, in a book whose author and title I cannot remember, the story of a father and his ten year-old daughter who were watching the news on TV, as they ate their dessert. At one point in the news a South African black man was forced out of his home by a group of youthful thugs. They followed him pelting him with stones and, finally, ended up stoning him to death. The little girl was quiet; then she asked: "Daddy, did this really happen or is this just make-believe on a TV show?" Somewhat uncomfortably, the father told her it was real. Her next question made him even more uncomfortable: "Daddy, why didn't the man with the camera help the person who was killed by the stones?"

This young girl's simple question evokes several other questions. Do camera persons and the other media people cease to be members of the human community when they are out seeking "an objective picture" of the news? Does their role relieve them of all human responsibility to those whose story they are telling? Are they simply innocent bystanders watching a crime unfold, with a concern just to tell the story, but, with no concern to involve themselves in the story?

A Reflection

Must we not say, not just about media people, but about ourselves, that those who see violence, injustice and dehumanizing actions lose their innocence if they fail to act and do what they can. They become guilty bystanders. If someone asks: where can we begin? Perhaps the simplest answer is: right where you are. Start with the people you rub elbows with every day. See them in God and as one with you in God. If everyone who reads this were to see this and if each of us moved another person to do the same, pockets of peace and harmony would spring up in many places, as people found in one another the unknown who is source of being and ground of love for us all.

Finding the World in God

I have a female friend whom I like to visit. I enjoy having her sit on my lap, as we have a friendly conversation. Her name is Katherine and she is two and a half years old. Last Christmas I gave her a stuffed toy shaped like a ball, 12 inches in diameter, representing the planet earth with its geological features of oceans and land masses, its various continents and countries. The toy was called "Hug a Planet."

After opening the gift, Katherine began to play with the "planet." She threw it about like a ball. She pushed it. She sat on it. She kicked it. But she didn't do much hugging. She has wonderful parents, however, and, when she gets older, she will begin to understand what planet earth is and why she should hug it. It's the only one we have.

As I watched Katherine putting her "planet" to uses it was never intended for, I could not help but think of how we adults, who should know better, are so much more abusive of planet earth than Katherine ever could be with her toy earth.

Perhaps the reason we tend to abuse the good earth that God gave us is that we see it as something outside us which we must dominate rather than a reality we are one with and therefore must treat with reverence. So easily we tend toward that forgetfulness of God and the fact that God is everywhere and that everything, the earth included, is in God. For like all of reality it is grounded in God and could not exist in separateness from God.

A Wonderful Prayer

Frequently in the Liturgy of the Hours, we have at morning prayer the *Benedicite* --that wonderful prayer from the book of Daniel, which calls upon all of creation to praise God. "Sun and moon, bless the Lord." "Cold and chill, bless the Lord." "Ice and snow, bless the Lord." Nights and days, light and darkness, mountains, hills, springs, rivers and dolphins and birds are all called upon to bless and praise the Lord. Priests, servants of God, holy men and women of humble heart --they too are called upon to bless and praise the Lord.

This wondrous canticle is a favorite of mine. I look forward to the times we say it in the liturgy. One of the reasons I like it is the contemplative spirit it exhibits. By that I mean, it doesn't divide created things into various classifications, as science does, for instance. It sees all created reality as one. The canticle is a great harmonious symphony of praise rising up from the one created world. It's sun and moon and stars and rivers and springs and men and women -- all in unison blessing and praising the source whence they came and the Ground of Love in which they continue to exist.

Jesus's Final Command

It is in this context of the unity of all created things that we must read Jesus' final command to his disciples just before his Ascension: "Go into the world (the cosmos) and proclaim the Good news of salvation to all creation." (Mk., 16:15) Note that the Gospel is to be proclaimed, not just to women and men, but to the whole of creation.

St. Francis of Assisi was doing a deeply symbolic thing when he preached to the birds. He was saying that, just as women and men had to be raised up from a fallen state, so too did the world of nature. The Gospel has to be proclaimed to all creation. As Paul puts it in the Epistle to the Romans: "The whole of creation has been groaning in travail," (8:22) as it awaits its own participation in the victory of Christ, as it awaits renewal. We are awakened by the Risen Christ to a consciousness of the unity of all creation and are called to proclaim that unity everywhere.

How Have We Done?

If we are honest we have to acknowledge that we have done a very poor job in proclaiming this oneness to all God's good creation. We have dissipated our natural resources. We have made it difficult for created nature to bless God. A polluted river or lake or ocean or a denuded forest is unable to offer proper praise to God. For it is not longer itself, no longer what God made it to be.

Controlling Our Technology

We have in wondrous ways built a technological world that ought to complement the good world that God gave us. But all too often our constructed world of steel and brick and concrete separates us from nature; and indeed the demands which our technological achievements impose on us have often proved destructive of the world of nature. We need to control our technology lest our desire to create our world destroy the world that God gave us.

Remember

As I have pointed out earlier, our greatest failing-- that which prevents us from showing the reverence we ought to the good things of the earth that should be praising God-- is our loss of awareness of the essential oneness of all of reality in God. We always seem to tend toward that spiritual apartheid that separates God from God's creation.

Thinking of Native Americans

It may be helpful, perhaps, to point out that the religious thinking of Native Americans can help us to recover this non-dualistic view of reality. These people who, long before our ancestors came, inhabited that part of planet earth which we now call our own, can teach us much about the oneness of all created things and the responsibility we have to reverence everything that is.

More than a hundred years ago the president of the United States, Millard Fillmore, wrote to a Native American chief, Chief Seattle. The President wanted to buy tribal land for settling new immigrants coming into the country. Chief Seattle wrote a moving reply to him:

> "The President in Washington sends word that he wishes to buy our land. But how can you buy or sell the sky? The land? The idea is strange to us. If we do not own the freshness of the air and the sparkle of the water, how can we sell them?
>
> Every part of the earth is sacred to my people. Every shining pine needle, every sandy shore... every meadow, every humming insect. All are holy in the memory and experience of my people.
>
> We know the sap which courses through the trees as we know the blood that courses through our veins. We are part of the earth and it is part of us. The perfumed flowers are our sisters. The bear, the deer, the great eagle, these are our brothers.

The shining water that moves in the streams and rivers is not just water, but the blood of our ancestors. If we sell you our land, you must remember that it is sacred... The water's murmur is the voice of my father's father...The rivers are our siblings. They quench our thirst, carry our canoes and feed our children. So you must give to the rivers the kindness you would give any brother or sister... You must remember that the air is precious to us... it shares its spirit with all the life it supports... [If we sell you our land] will you teach your children what we have taught our children? That the earth is our mother? What befalls the earth befalls all the children of earth...

This we know; the earth does not belong to us; we belong to the earth. All things are connected like the blood that unites us all... Our God is also your God. The earth is precious to God and to harm the earth is to heap contempt on its creator...

We love the earth as a newborn loves its mother's heartbeat. So if we sell you our land, love it as we have loved it...Preserve the land for all children and love it, as God loves us all..."

  Several years ago I gave a retreat at the Columbian retreat house in Derby, New York. The retreat was centered around the theme that has run through this chapter, namely, awareness of God and the consciousness of the oneness of all reality in God. One of the women making the retreat came to see me and told me: "I have no problem whatever with what you have been saying about the unity of all reality. That has always been a part of my thinking." She went on to tell me that for a long time she had felt strange about thinking this way, as most of her friends didn't seem to understand it at all. Then she explained that she was an orphan and had only recently learned that she had been born of Native American parents. She went on further to say that she had always had difficulty with Jesus' words in the Gospel where he tells us: "You are of more value than many sparrows." (Mt. 10:31) "Sparrows," she said, "are just as much God's good creatures as we are." I thanked her for sharing that perception with me. I also pointed out to her that perhaps Jesus also shared it, more than she realized. For he also said: "Not one sparrow falls to the ground without your Father's will." "Go into the world and proclaim the Gospel to all creation." Don't allow yourselves, Jesus tells us, to drift into forgetfulness and lack of awareness. Remember, sparrows matter. So do rivers and lakes and trees and flowers. So does the good air which God has given us. So do people everywhere on the earth. Perhaps this final command of Jesus to bring the unifying word of salvation to all creation could be summed up in those simple, all-embracing words (whose meaning my little friend Katherine will some day learn): "Hug a planet!

Discovering and Remembering God's Presence

Contemplative spirituality is strongly non-dualistic. Non-dualism means non- separateness. It means that, while I am distinct from God, I am not separate from God. When I discover God I discover myself and at the same time when I discover myself I discover God. For I find myself in God. There is nowhere else that I can find myself. This is true not only of me, it is true of every human being who exists. The implications of this wondrous truth for involvement in the life of the church is tremendous. For if I am one with God and my brothers and sisters are one with God, then we are all one with one another. When I touch their lives I touch God and I touch my own true self. For wherever reality is there is God. When we begin to understand this tremendous truth, we suddenly realize that at every moment of our lives we are in the situation of prayer, for we are in the presence of God.

We don't have to place ourselves in the presence of God, as we used to say in beginning our prayers, because that is where we always and necessarily are. We do not turn away from the world in order to find God, as if God were somehow outside it; rather in finding God we discover in a new way our world, and especially our sisters and brothers in it. Our real problem in prayer is not getting ourselves into God's presence -- we are always there -- but the strange fact that our sense of the presence of God is continually slipping from our memory. And of course forgetfulness of the presence of God is not like ordinary forgetfulness, like forgetting where you put your car keys or forgetting someone's birthday, for example. The first may curtail your driving for the time being and the second may put you in someone's bad graces. But forgetting about the presence of God is forgetting about the context and setting of all reality. It is forgetting what is essential to my very being and to that of everything that exists. It is forgetting what is truly real.

Forgetfulness

We are so prone to this forgetfulness that we can be forgetful of God even when we pray, as when we pray to a God who is distant from us rather than to the God in whom we are, in whom we live, and move and have our being.

Forgetting the presence of God can have repercussions in our relationships with our sisters and brothers and all of the world, for it can lead us to ignore the sacredness and dignity of every person and indeed everything that God has made. After all, we and they are all one in God. But when we forget the presence of God, we forget this fundamental oneness. We see others as separate, not as they really are: one with us and one with one another because all are one in God. To be aware of God is to understand the deepest roots of human intimacy and communion. This forgetfulness of our oneness with God is not just a personal experience, it is the corporate experience of humanity. Indeed, this is one way of understanding original sin. We are in God, but we don't seem to know it, we are in paradise, but we don't realize it.

     The mystical picture of paradise described in Genesis suggests that the man and woman were one with God, walking with God in the cool of the evening. They were one with the rest of reality. All was harmony and peace. The fall is the fall from the oneness and harmony of paradise into disunity, alienation, and a sense of separation. Humanity has fallen not into the real world, but a world of illusions and unreality. We no longer see things as they truly are. Where there is oneness we see separateness where there is harmony we see alienation and manipulation of people. It is not so much that this oneness is taken away. It is present in us, hidden in the depths of our being, but it lies there forgotten. What Jesus does in redeeming us is to wake us from the sleep of separateness. He rouses us from the forgetfulness of unity so that we recover what was always there.

The Contemplative and the Community

I invite you to recall the letter from the woman in the Southwest who felt that her reading of Merton had freed her from the guilt she experienced in her life. Merton's writings did this by helping her to see that she was called to the contemplative life. I see her as a symbol of literally thousands of people who have undergone similar experiences through their reading of Merton. I have tried to describe what has happened to her or is happening to her in contemplation as, in her words, "she continues her journey toward wholeness as a layperson." She said that she had received permission from her own spirit, which makes a great deal of sense. For contemplation builds a unity in us and gives us the inner resources to make decisions about our lives and actions in freedom and peace. A contemplative is not one who spurns contact with the Christian community. The contemplative loves that community and assumes a share of responsibility for its welfare. The contemplative listens to the wisdom of the Christian community and to the voice of authority in the community, willingly and gratefully, but not with an attitude of supine submission.

As Merton wrote to Etta Gullick: "A contemplative is one who has God's will bearing straight down on him or her, often in the most incomprehensible ways." The contemplative understands, and in some mysterious way experiences, those remarkable words we find in the first epistle of John:

> 'you have the anointing that comes from the holy one so that all knowledge is yours… the anointing you received from him remains in

your hearts. This means you have no need for anyone to teach you. Rather as his anointing teaches you about all things and is true -- free from any lie -- remain in him, as he taught you to do.'

This is not an antinomian statement nor is it a form of Quietism. It is rather a statement of Christian freedom and theonomous decision making. The contemplative is able to stand on his or her own feet and accept personal responsibility before God for his or her thoughts and actions.

In the final talk of his life, which he gave in Bangkok, Thomas Merton tells the story of a Tibetan abbot who had to flee for his life when the Chinese overran Tibet. He sent a message to a nearby abbot friend of his asking: "What do we do?" The abbot sent back this message: "From now on, brother, everybody stands on his (her) own feet." Merton points out that this is "an important statement about Christianity, if you understand it in terms of grace." It is not, he insists, a discouraging statement, by any means, but his statement to the effect that we can no longer rely on being supported by structures that may be destroyed at any moment.

A spiritually mature person, while needing to listen to the wisdom of the Christian community and the authority in the community, still has the responsibility, which cannot be advocated to another of standing on his or her own feet in accepting personal responsibility before God for his or her own actions. This is a true freedom that comes with a developed contemplative spirituality.

So many people are searching for this kind of authentic interior life through the writings of Thomas Merton. He may have called himself a mud pile but he has proved to be a rock of stability for countless numbers of people who have found in his writings a spirituality that offers them depth, unity, and freedom.

A Question to the Reader

At this point I want to put a question to the reader. The question is: are you satisfied with the way you pray? I had put this question to many people to whom I have given retreats. I have never heard anyone say: Yes, I pray very well. And they would mean it. It would not be like other situations that might come up in which persons might think it proper to make a self derogatory statements. For instance you might say to someone who plays the piano well: "You play very well." Or you might say to an artist: "Your work is sensational." They might reply: "That's kind of you but I am not really that good at it. They would say something like that because they figured that modesty required that they say it, but what they're really saying inside: "You better believe it; "I really do play well or I am a fine artist." At least I believe it when people say I don't pray well. For you know they really mean it. It is not false modesty. It is just what they think is true, they really believe that they do not pray well.

In the context of all that I have said about contemplative prayer I want to try to remove from people's minds the notion that they don't pray well. Remember Father Flanagan and Boys Town (if you do, you will probably also remember the great football team they used to have). Father Flanagan used to say that there is no such thing as a bad boy. In terms of what I have said about contemplative prayer I hope I have spoken a word of comfort for those who feel they don't pray well. For I want to say there is no such thing as a bad prayer.

Perhaps the following remarkable quotation from Merton's book, *The New Man,* will be a brief summary of what he had to say about prayer.

> The experience of contemplation
> Is the experience of God's life and presence
> within ourselves
> Not as an object, but as the transcendent source
> of our own subjectivity
> Contemplation is a mystery
> In which God reveals Himself to us
> At the very center of our own most intimate
> self-
> *Interior intimo meo* as Augustine said.
> When the realization of his presence bursts
> upon us,
> Our own self disappears in Him,
> And we pass mystically through the Red Sea of
> separation
> To lose ourselves (and thus find our true
> selves) in Him.

(This has been arranged in sense sentences.)

CHAPTER THREE

MY CONVERSION TO A NEW WAY OF UNDERSTANDING PEACE MAKING AND NON-VIOLENCE

"Christ our Lord brought to his disciples a vocation and a task; to struggle in the world of violence to establish His peace not only in our own hearts but in society itself."

Thus far I have tried to show how Merton was an important factor in shaping American Catholic Spirituality. But contemplation not only unites us with God and with one another. It also calls us to new responsibilities. In his day Merton believed that one important task that contemplation demands of us is to work for peace and non-violence. The time that Merton came to realize this responsibility was a time when work for peace was not an uppermost commitment in the lives of most Catholics. His writings on peace helped to shape the Catholic Peace Movement.

In the autumn of 1961 Thomas Merton made a decision that would profoundly affect his own future and the future reception his writings would receive from a large public which, for more than a decade, had listened so intently to what this monk had to say about prayer and contemplation. For the many thousands who had read *The Seven Storey Mountain, Seeds of Contemplation, The Sign of Jonas, No Man is An Island,* Merton had become a spiritual director through the pages of his books.

A wide readership eagerly waited for what might be his newest insight on the spiritual life. Many of these devoted followers did not realize, however, the transformation that had been going on in his life: a transformation that would lead to what can only be called the **momentous decision of October 1961**. Perhaps he scarcely realized it himself. The transformation he was experiencing was an outgrowth of his prayer and contemplation. His solitude had issued into what all true solitude must eventually become: compassion. Finding God in his solitude, he found God's people who were inseparable from God and who, at the deepest level of their being (the level that only contemplation can reach), are at one with one another in-God, the Hidden Ground of Love of all that is.

New Thinking

This sense of compassion bred in solitude (something like the *karuna* of the Buddha born of his enlightenment) moved him to look once again at the world he thought he had left irrevocably in 1941 when he had entered the monastery. Now 21 years later, in 1961, he felt a duty to speak out to that world and warn the women and men of his day against what he considered the gravest possible danger that threatened the civilized world. He had come to realize that being a monk was no justification for dodging the responsibility he shared with the whole human race: the responsibility of dealing with the problems of women and men of his day.

If readers are wondering why I am emphasizing Merton's change from a life of withdrawal from the world to one of responsibility for his role in the world, I can only say that Merton's experience paralleled something that was happening to me. It is not that I entered a monastery, but my continued reading of Merton and my reflection on what he had to say about contemplation and how contemplation led him eventually to a non-violent reaching out to the world.

The Just War Movement

For much of my life I have been a strong defender of the Just War Theory. It was a theory that was developed, not out of the scriptures, but out of a situation that existed in the Christian world after the time of Constantine. The period after Constantine was a time in the history of the church when the followers of Jesus made every effort to live out Jesus' call that we love one another. The Just War Theory was developed as a way whereby people could deal with violence, but only in fulfilling certain conditions. For instance, one of the principles was that the means of defense must not exceed the wrong that had been done. Also one had to love the enemy, something that surely seems an impossibility. The conditions for the Just War were developed by Christian leaders like Saint Ambrose and Saint Augustine. It must be said, however, that they do not include the non-violent love that Jesus teaches in the Gospels. Still the Just War Theory continued to be the guiding approach to war for Christian for 2000 years. It was not until the mid 20th Century that Christians began to understand and apply Jesus' teachings on non-violence. That this has become an acceptable Christian approach to dealing with war was taught by the Second Vatican Council.

Merton was part of a group of Christian leaders who fostered non-violence as the only way of dealing with the scourge of war.

Merton's Mission Statement

On November 10, 1958 Merton wrote a letter to Pope John XXIII, in which he said:

> "It seems to me that as a contemplative, I do not need to lock myself into solitude and lose contact with the rest of the world, rather this poor world has a right to a place in my solitude. It is not enough for me to think of the Apostolic value of prayer and penance; I also have to think in terms of a contemplative grasp of the political, intellectual, artistic and social movements in this world - by which I mean a sympathy for the honest aspirations of so many

intellectuals in the world and the terrible problems they have to face." He goes on to say that he has had many contacts with people who are artists, writers, poets, etc., "Who have become my friends without my having to leave the cloistered. I have exercised an apostolate- small and limited though it be - within a circle of intellectuals from other parts of the world. It has been quite simply an apostolate of friendship."

This may be seen as his mission statement that led him to write more boldly about war and peace.

Silence in the Church about the Issue of War

Writing on August 22, 1961 to Dorothy Day-- the one person the was sure would take to heart the decision he was in process of making-- telling her that he feels "obligated to take very seriously what is going on, and to say whatever my conscience dictates." He makes clear to her the difficult dilemma that might be forced upon him. He puts the question --more to himself than to her -- as to what one should do in a situation "where obedience would completely silence a person on some important issue on which others are also keeping silence -a crucial issue like nuclear war." For that was the issue that was so much on his mind. He wonders whether being forced into silence by obedience would require a person of good conscience to change his/her life-situation. As if answering his own question, he says he has no thought of leaving the monastery and professes his faith that God has somehow always seemed to make it possible for him to say what it appeared necessary for him to say.

Yet, he is keenly aware of the loneliness in which such a situation places him. "Why," he asks, "this awful silence on the part of Catholics, clergy, hierarchy, lay people on this terrible issue on which the very continued existence of the human race depends?"

Why this awful silence?" he asked. And there really was silence in the Catholic community in the early 1960s on the question of war. The only group that strongly condemned war was the Catholic Worker and they were looked upon with suspicion by many Catholics. Some even thought them to be communists. Apart from the historical peace churches (the Quakers, the Mennonites and the Brethren), the only organized peace group in the United States was the *Fellowship of Reconciliation. The Fellowship* was considered a Protestant organization, which meant --in the extremely unecumenical atmosphere that prevailed in the early sixties, no Catholic would think of joining it (though Merton actually did join in 1962).

Yet so strong were his convictions that, even if he had to do it alone, he would still speak out. Though all others remained silent, his conscience would not allow him to do so. And if proof were needed that the monk who wrote earlier with such eloquence about the contemplative life was thinking in new directions (though I would want to say that these new directions were not a disavowal of his contemplative spirituality, but an outgrowth of it), he goes on, in this letter to Dorothy Day:

> I don't feel that I can in conscience go on writing just about things like meditation, though that has its point. I cannot just bury my head in a lot of tiny and secondary monastic studies either. I think I have to face the big

issues, the life-and-death issues: and this is what everyone is afraid of. So do please pray that I may find God's way through the labyrinth and pick my steps as he wants me to and do what is His will, and avoid too much silly conflict and argumentation.

It is clear that the decision Merton was struggling with was extremely important to him, though one senses-- from the tone of his letter-- that he was not so much asking for Dorothy's advice, but thinking through a decision he had already made, and doing so in a letter to someone he was sure would be sympathetic with that decision.

An Anguished Decision

It was this kind of thinking, which had been going on in his mind for some time, that finally moved Thomas Merton to "cross the Rubicon" and set his life decisively on a new path from which there would be no returning. He made *the big decision of October 1961;* the decision to go public in speaking out against war and against what he described as the "war fever" in America.

To understand the momentous character of this decision, we must try to grasp something of the anguish that this choice brought him. We live at a time when it is not an uncommon thing for Roman Catholics to protest against war and to lobby for peace. While certainly not a majority in the Catholic Church, such persons are still respected for their commitment to conscience.

Some fifty years ago, in 1961, the situation was quite different. No Catholic Peace Movement existed. No Catholic priest or bishop --at least none well known --had raised his voice against war. Certainly no monk had done so. Merton was a well-known Catholic priest and monk, whose reputation had been established by his writings on spirituality --writings which lauded withdrawal from the world as much as possible and which gave scarcely a hint that their author would ever speak out on such a worldly subject as war or even think of issuing a call to abolish all war.

Furthermore, the ecclesiastical situation in the Catholic Church in 1961 was anything but congenial to the establishment of a strong peace movement. Francis Cardinal Spellman was archbishop of New York. He had the ear of the Vatican. He "called the shots" in the American Church. His influence was powerful. And he was the Bishop Ordinary for the American armed forces. Pax Christi USA, which today represents the largest Catholic peace group in this country, did not, of course, exist at that time. In fact it could not have existed.

The reason I say it could not have exist is that one of the requirements for establishing a national Pax Christi movement is that there be a bishop as president. No Catholic Bishop emerged at that time or for some considerable time after. Pax Christi USA celebrated its 20th anniversary last year. This means that it did not come into being until 1972. And it is no accident that this was four years after Thomas Gumbleton was ordained auxiliary bishop of Detroit. In 1972, four years after his ordination as a bishop, Gumbleton became the first bishop sponsor of Pax Christi. He made it possible for Pax Christi to exist in the United States.

In 1961, therefore, when Merton decided to raise his voice against war, he was practically a one-man peace movement. There were no Bishop Gumbletons around; and American Catholic culture was strong in patriotism and committed to the belief that what was good for America was good for the world. If America went to war it was taken for granted that it would always be in a good cause. There was a sense of righteousness and an almost childlike innocence that American showered on their country. We had not yet gotten into the quagmire of Viet Nam--the war in which America lost its sense of innocence and joined the company of nations tainted by war's injustices and needing to repent and be renewed. It is worth pointing out, in passing, that this year of Merton's decision, 1961 saw the first commitment of U.S. support troops to the Diem government in Viet Nam.

Standing Alone

Merton's action, then, was one that required great courage: the courage to risk standing alone. He was to write later to Ernesto Cardenal, *The Courage for Truth* that when one is opposing power-systems, "it is very good, almost essential to have at one's side others with a similar determination...A completely isolated witness is much more difficult and dangerous." This sounds very much like the voice of experience: the voice of one who in 1961 had to begin the struggle against war alone, without others at his side. Was it at this time in 1961 that he came to realize the truth that he would speak later in 1968 at Bangkok in what were, significantly, his last words to us: "From now on, Brother, everyone has to learn to stand on his own feet." [which I quoted earlier]

Planning the Carrying Out of the Decision

Besides this courage to stand alone, the carrying out of his decision to oppose war also required careful planning to carry it off properly. All his monastic life Merton had to deal with the censors of his Order whose duty it was to determine not just the **orthodoxy of what he wrote, but also its**

appropriateness. So he planned his strategy very carefully. Put yourself in his position. Suppose you had a reputation for being unworldly --a person of prayer--and you wanted to get an article published that would have to be passed by censors who would probably take a rigid view of what it was appropriate for you to publish, --where would you be inclined to put such an article? Obviously the best place to hide it would be somewhere in the middle of a book on prayer. This is exactly what Merton did.

In 1961 he had undertaken an extensive revision of an earlier (rather naive) book on prayer, called *Seeds of Contemplation*. In the considerably revised, and vastly improved, text (called *New Seeds of Contemplation*) he lengthened and strengthened a chapter that bore the title "The Root of War is Fear." There was nothing startling about the chapter, certainly nothing in it that one might not expect a contemplative monk to say. **It was all right for monks to be opposed to war in general.** The book was passed by the censors.

The Catholic Worker of October 1961

Immediately upon receiving the censors' approval and several months before the book would get into print, Merton sent this chapter to Dorothy Day for publication in the *Catholic Worker*. It was published immediately, in the October 1961 issue. It is at this point that the web of Mertonian intrigue begins to be spun. To the version of this chapter that had been accepted by the censors, Merton added three very long paragraphs --which of course the censors never saw. (He was just being considerate. After all, he did not want to inconvenience them by sending the manuscript to them a second time!)He suggested to Dorothy Day that these paragraphs might be placed at the beginning of the article. Their purpose, he told her, somewhat casually, was simply to situate his thoughts in the context of the present crisis in the world.

It is difficult to be sure whether Merton was being naive or clever or just plain reckless. At any rate, these "situating paragraphs" were highly inflammatory (in a way that the chapter of the book was not). So tightly and passionately written were they that it is hardly an exaggeration to say that they sum up in brief and almost brilliant fashion a whole program for opposing war and working for peace.

The Uncensored Paragraphs

The uncensored paragraphs begin with the description of an illness --a war-fever -- that has swept through the world. He sees the whole world plunging headlong into frightful destruction and "doing so with the *purpose of avoiding war and preserving peace!* Of all the sick countries of the world he singles out his own adopted country, the United States, as the most grievously afflicted. In an imaginative picture he describes people building bomb shelters, where they will simply bake slowly instead of being blown out of existence in a flash. He fantasizes that people will even sit at the entrance to their shelters with machine guns to prevent their neighbor from entering. And this, he asks, is a nation that claims to be fighting for religious truth and freedom and other values of the spirit? "Truly we have entered the 'post-Christian era' with a vengeance."

He went on to discuss the duty of the Christian in the present situation. We must not embrace a fatalistic attitude, much less the madness of the warmongers who would calculate how by a first strike the glorious Christian West could eliminate atheistic communism for all time. This sabre-rattling attitude he sees as "the great and not, even subtle, temptation of a Christianity that has grown rich and comfortable..." In a more positive vein he insists that the one duty that every Christian must assume in this critical time is the task of working for the total abolition of war. Otherwise the world will remain in a state of madness and desperation, in which, "because of the immense destructive power of modern weapons, the danger of catastrophe will be imminent..."

Addressing the responsibility of the Church, he says that, while the Church does not always have clear answers regarding precise strategies, "she must lead the way on the road toward non-violent settlement of difficulties and toward the gradual abolition of war as the way of settling international or civil disputes." There is also much that must be done by individual Christians: much to be studied, much to be learned. Peace is to be preached. Non-violence is to be explained as a practical method. There is need for prayer and sacrifice. At a deep internal level we have to overcome the hidden aggressions that often express themselves in our relationships; and we must commit ourselves to work for the truth and not just for results.

We may never succeed in this campaign, but whether we succeed or not, the duty is evident. It is the great Christian task of our time. Everything else is secondary, for the survival of the human race itself depends upon it...

This article in the October 1961 issue of *The Catholic Worker* marked what I have called Merton's "official" entrance into the peace movement. It came as a surprise to most people: a joyous surprise to the handful of Catholics, like *The Catholic Worker* people, who had labored in this area with little recognition from their correligionists; a disconcerting surprise for a great many Catholics, including some members of the American Catholic hierarchy, who felt that this "good monk" should give his life to prayer and leave the conduct of the affairs of the "world" to those who were more knowledgeable. Most of those who belonged to the second group would not, for the most part, be regular readers of *The Catholic Worker;* hence it would have been some time later, when his articles began to appear in more widely read journals, that people came to realize that a "new Merton" had appeared on the scene.

Origin of the Cold War Letters

October 1961, or at least the fall of 1961, is an important time in Merton's lonesome crusade against war, not only because it was the date of his first article on war, but also because it was at this time that he conceived the plan of putting together a new type of book that would have far-reaching influence in the struggle against war. The book he conceived at that time was one that would be made up of selected letters of his own, written to a wide variety of people, but linked together by the common theme that they all addressed: some aspect of the war-peace issue. Not only did he conceive the book, he also decided on a title: The *Cold War Letters*.

It was a cleverly conceived plan; for it was a way in which Merton could spread his ideas broadcast without too much adverse publicity coming his way. The letters could get to the "right" people who would be sympathetic with his position and do something to implement it; at the same time there would be minimal risk of his material getting into the hands of those who would find it most objectionable to find Merton saying the kind of things he was writing.

Merton probably made the decision to have such a book printed about the same time as his *Catholic Worker* article appeared. One of my reasons for making this judgment is that the letters he selected begin with October of 1961 and cease with October of 1962. A second reason that would also appear to confirm this judgment may be found in a letter which Merton wrote on December 21, 1961 to Dr. Wilbur H. ("Ping") Ferry of the Santa Barbara Center for the Study of Democratic Institutions. He asked Ferry if he would be willing to circulate some of his material in mimeographed form. "I am having a bit of censorship trouble," he remarked, somewhat casually.

He made clear that getting his "stuff" around in this clandestine way would not require prior censorship. He then mentions *The Cold War Letters* for the first time, as an example of material that could be circulated in this private fashion. "I have, for instance," he writes, "some copies of letters to people -to make up a book called *Cold War Letters*. Very unlikely to be published (!)." (HGL, 203) At the time this letter was written, Merton would have had only eleven of the letters that would eventually go into the Cold War collection of letters, yet the volume of *Cold War Letters,* finally printed in mimeographed form, consisted of 49 letters in its early edition and 111 in the later printing.

The Cold War Letters, then, were not -- as many have believed-- an after-thought that came to Merton after he had been forbidden to write publicly on the topic of war and peace. Quite the contrary, the idea of such a volume of letters was a part of his thinking almost from the moment he decided to enter the struggle against war. They were an important instrument in that struggle. They circulated in mimeographed form in the famous yellow cover with the title and the warning:

"Confidential, Not for Publication." [I might add, in parenthesis, that they have appeared in published form, published by Orbis.]

Quite a number of copies of *The Cold War Letters* in the famous yellow cover circulated during Merton's lifetime. During the Second Vatican Council copies got to Rome and into the hands of various bishops. Merton personally sent copies to some of the bishops, including Bishop Wright of Pittsburgh. He also sent copies to the well known theologian Bernard Haring. He also sent them to a group of women, under the leadership of Dorothy Day and Hildegard Goss-Mayr, who were in Rome lobbying for peace. It is tempting to think that this work, as well as Merton's other writings on war and peace, exerted a positive influence on the Council Fathers when they came to write the section (articles 77-82) on war and peace in *Gaudium et Spes* (The Pastoral Constitution on the Church in the Modern World). The Bishops' statement that the nuclear age forces us to reevaluate war with an entirely new mentality, the praise they give to those who choose the way of non-violence, their condemnation of total war, their disapproval of the arms' race as a deterrent to war, their urgent call to all peoples "to strain every muscle as we work for the time when all war can be completely outlawed by international consent." (art. 82). These stances resonate with positions on these issues that Merton had taken in his articles and in the *Cold War Letters*.

The *Catholic Worker* article of October 1961 was followed not only by the *Cold War Letters*, but by a barrage of essays appearing in a variety of journals: *Commonweal, Jubilee, Fellowship, Blackfriars,* but mostly in *The Catholic Worker*. It was a time of enormous anxiety for Merton. Because he was practically alone, he was sensitive to whatever criticisms were being made of the position he took. He did his best to answer these criticisms. Some of the Cold War letters are precisely that: responses to people who disagreed with him. Some of his articles are re-writes of previous articles, as Merton's anxiety moved him to make continued efforts to make his position as clear as possible.

The *Commonweal* Article of February 9, 1962

Probably the single most important essay he wrote on the war issue was an essay for *Commonweal*. It has been commissioned for the Christmas 1961 issue, but --because it was held up by the censors--it did not get into print till February 9, 1962. In the article he speaks of a *moral passivity* that refuses to face the gravity of the danger at stake for the whole human race. At the same time there is a *demonic activism* at work which has so perfected weaponry technology that the world is plunging to disaster with such furious speed that no one, including political leaders, is any longer fully in command. We are at the mercy, not just of the malice of the wicked, but the helpless futility of the "good." Christians must make themselves heard;

> "Ambiguity, hesitation and compromise are no longer permissible. War must be abolished. A world government must be established. We have still time to do something about it, but the time is rapidly running out."

The delay of the censors in approving this article, was a harbinger of even stiffer opposition that was to come. As Merton's articles became more incisive, the censors became more uncomfortable. In the spring of 1962 he wrote the draft of an article called "Target Equals City," in which he showed the folly of believing that our national policy was only counterforce. Military plans included cities, he asserted --cities where there were no combatants and no military installations. He documents with proof that the choice of Hiroshima as the place for the dropping of the first nuclear bomb was not dictated by any military reason. It was the deliberate choice of a city. Indeed, President Truman had ordered the drawing up of a list of cities. The list actually included Kyoto, a sacred city in Japan. Bombing it would be like bombing Jerusalem or Mecca or Rome. Fortunately, Truman had a Secretary of State who knew enough to say "no" to Kyoto. The next choice was Hiroshima.

The Ax Falls: The Abbot General's Prohibition

The censor refused outright to give his approval to "Target Equals City". Merton, he claimed, was entering into controversial areas in a way that was contrary to the statutes of the Order. But, more than that, his argumentation was fallacious. Merton had insisted that Pope Pius XII had repeatedly insisted on the traditional principle that the rights of unarmed and non-combatant civilians must be respected and that *failure to take these into account is a grave crime.* The censor, while agreeing on the principle of the rights of innocent civilians, still insists that the Pope had never given the impression that these rights would prevail over a nation's right to self-defense. This latter right might even justify the use of atomic weapons.

This is the way the censor, who was himself a theologian of the Order, read the writings of the Pope. It was not the way Merton read them. It is obvious that Merton was on a collision course with the authorities of the Order. And in April of 1962 the ax fell. Dom James Fox, Merton's abbot, informed him that Gabriel Sortais, the Abbot General of the entire Order, had ordered Merton to cease publishing on the topic of war and peace. In fact, he was not even to submit material for censorship on these topics.

Understandably Merton was discouraged. But by this time he was used to working within structures that change very slowly. A year later, on May 13, 1963, he wrote to Helen Wolff:

> "Unfortunately I am now in a position where I am not allowed to publish on the issue of war and peace. Isn't that absurd? Especially when the encyclical (Pacem in Terris) has come out with exactly what I was saying. It is wearying to have to work in a great slow moving structure like "this..."

There is a good bit of autobiography in that last sentence: "It is wearying to have to work in a great slow moving structure like this."

Criticism Outside the Order

This whole new direction in Merton's writings bothered the censors. It bothered his critics too. Bishop Hannan, auxiliary of Washington D.C. (later archbishop of New Orleans) attacked his *Commonweal a*rticle in the Washington diocesan paper, *The Standard.* He was also criticized in the letters to the editor of *Commonweal.* It is probably fair to say too that this new trend in his writings bothered some of his readers. The interest in Merton and his thought , which *Seven Storey Mountain, The Sign of Jonas* and other early writings had enkindled, cooled noticeably in this period and the popularity of his writings waned for a time.

Understandably, for he had entered an area that was not congenial to those who had been his faithful readers. A fairly extreme instance of this sort of reaction came from the British writer, Auberon Waugh, whose father, Evelyn Waugh, had prepared the British edition of *Seven Storey Mountain*. It was quite a bit later that Auberon Waugh, in reviewing Monica Furlong's biography of Merton for the London *Telegraph*, stumbled upon this "new" Merton. He was shocked by what he read of Merton's later years. His review speaks with obvious relish of the monastery Merton had entered, where, as he put it: "Their diet was sparse and nasty; they slept on pallets in a dormitory...had no heating in winter, no contact with the outside world, and were expected to scourge themselves from time to time...Not the sort of life you or I might choose [he confides to his readers] but jolly interesting to read about in others. It was gratifying, too, [he added] to learn that these people were doing it all to atone for our sins."

Then, to his dismay, Waugh discovers in Monica Furlong's biography that everything had changed. Merton had gotten his own special hermitage, where he played Bob Dylan records, had all sorts of visitors and used to go to Louisville to drink rum punch with his friends. Waugh was scandalized. He asks:

> "What are we to make of this rubbish --that Merton had gone mad? That he was suffering from the enfeeblement of the brain which affected many Americans at this time...Or perhaps is it simply time to admit that we were wrong about his earlier book --that he was not a deeply spiritual man at all, but merely one of those unhappy confused people who seem to

abound in the United States, emerging from their obscurity only when they pause to murder President Kennedy or John Lennon or about 500 fellow citizens."

Quite clearly, no one could accuse Auberon Waugh of being pro-American or pro-Merton. Others were not quite as vituperous as Waugh, but it is true that many who had followed Merton so eagerly in the 1950s began looking elsewhere for spiritual guidance.

The Smallest and Most Neglected of Movements

But this loss of readership was compensated for by the gain of a whole new readership: namely, the increasing number of people who had become social activists and advocates of peace and who now found that *they* could look to Merton for guidance. Indeed many who embraced that role did so because of Merton's influence. More than any other Catholic leader of the time, he was the one, I believe, who shaped the American Catholic Peace Movement. That movement grew from very small and not particularly auspicious beginnings. Merton wrote to Ernesto Cardenal (December 24, 1961) that the peace movement was the "smallest and the most neglected of 'movements' in the whole Church." Initially it was for the most part in the hands of young people, who had glimpsed a vision worth working for, but were immature and undisciplined in their lives. They were committed to non-violence, but they were not always very sure what it meant. On one occasion a number of them connected with the *Catholic Worker* put out a risque edition of the *Worker,* which of course never got circulated, but which caused Dorothy Day a great deal of pain and concern. They did not see that this apparent act of fun was in reality an act of violence. Merton often lamented their immaturity and was constantly warning those people who felt themselves called to non-violence to beware of the hidden aggressions in themselves. He also insisted with them that non-violence was a commitment to the truth, not necessarily to results. Thus he wrote to Martin Corbin, editor of the magazine *Liberation* of the "necessity for complete 'purity' in our non-violent action: complete detachment from results."

> "We must act only because the act itself is true, and expresses the truth. We must not even demand that the truth be immediately recognized. Still less must we expect to be congratulated. On the contrary, it may well mean a cracked skull. This purity of action is the fundamental guarantee of its truth. It is the only thing that gives the non-violent demonstrator power against the mass media with all their money and all their influence. As for results: the truth needs only to be manifested. It can take care of itself."(December 1961)

On another occasion Jim Forest wrote to him saying he was discouraged. The peace movement didn't seem to be getting anywhere. Merton wrote a very moving letter to him enunciating this same principle about non-violence.

> "Do not depend on the hope of results. When you are doing the sort of work you have taken on...you may have to face the fact that your work will be apparently worthless and even achieve no results at all...As you get used to this idea you start more and more to concentrate not on the results but on the value, the rightness, the truth

of the work itself...you struggle less and less for an idea and more and more for specific people...It is the reality of personal relationships that saves everything." (*HGL*, 294)

November 1964: Retreat at Gethsemani for Peace

In November 1964 Merton carried out a project that would have important results for the future. He brought together for a retreat at Gethsemani a number of people involved in the work for peace. It was an ecumenical gathering. In attendance were A. J. Muste, perhaps the most venerated of all those involved in the peace movement, also Daniel and Philip Berrigan, James Forest, John Howard Yoder, John Nelson, Wilbur H. Ferry, Thomas Cornell, Tony Walsh (from Montreal). The topic of the retreat was: "Our common grounds for Religious Dissent and Commitment in the Face of Injustice and Disorder." The discussions went on from Wednesday, November 18 to Friday, November 20. Merton led the discussions on Wednesday; Muste and Yoder on Thursday and Daniel Berrigan on Friday. To my knowledge there is, unfortunately, no detailed reporting of this retreat. One of the works that was discussed at great length was the just published translation of Jacques Ellul's book on technology, The *Technological Society*.

Moving Toward "Questionable" Tactics?

In October 1967 some members of the fledgling peace movement believed they should move in a new direction. Daniel Berrigan wrote to Merton asking him for his reflections on what he and his brother Phil felt was that new direction. It was their conviction that, while preserving a stance of non-violence toward persons, violence could legitimately be directed at *idolatrous things*, such as draft records or implements of destruction. Merton was quite obviously uncomfortable with this approach. He writes a very pastoral approach which shows his respect for them, but his very obvious uneasiness in seeing the peace movement move in a direction that would countenance some form of violence. "It is definitely outside the Gandhian way," he said; "and I believe that some of us should stay with Gandhi's approach." We have to avoid getting hung up on "merely futile moral posturing." We have to make choices and "the most popular and exciting thing at the moment is not necessarily the best choice." He questioned the value of a symbol whose meaning was lost on most people.

Writing to a woman from Princeton in June of 1968, he says quite clearly: "As to the Berrigan brothers, they are friends of mine. I don't agree with their methods of action, but I can understand the desperation which prompts them."

I have been able to touch on but a few aspects of Merton's role in the building of the American Catholic Peace Movement. Today, in 2011, that movement, thanks in great part to Thomas Merton, has attained a certain maturity and respectability. People involved in it are no longer looked upon as subversives or odd-balls. As the terrible devastation wrought by war --which Merton wrote about so passionately-- becomes increasingly evident, the number of those committed to the total abolition of war continues to grow. Just after the War against Sadam Hussein a publication emanating from Rome and probably voicing Vatican positions came as close as any ecclesiastical document has to condemning all war and declaring the "just war" theory obsolete. But all this was something Merton was not to know in his life time.

As far as his reading public is concerned today, I think it is fair to say that the two groups--the "prayer" people and the "action" people- have managed to embrace one another, as the fundamental unity of prayer and action in Merton's mature writings have become clear. Contemplation and social engagement go together: they cannot exist, in any truly authentic form, in separation from one another. This is the point of the title of a posthumously published book of Merton's called *Contemplation in a World of Action*.

Peace Movement and Contemplation

I would simply point out that it was contemplation that led Merton to the realization that he had to oppose war and, further, that it was his responsibility to encourage all peoples of good will to do the same. In contemplation he had experienced his own oneness with God and the oneness in God of all peoples and indeed of all reality. Violence and the ultimate violence, war, obscure that oneness and make us believe that it doesn't really exist. For a contemplative then, war is the ultimate illusion: not in the sense that it doesn't exist, but in the sense that it seeks to blind people to the most important fact of reality: the unity of humankind in God. War perpetuates, therefore, the ultimate illusion. It places us in a world of separateness and alienation --a world that in ultimate terms is not the real world at all. War is the ultimate symbol of the Fall from paradise. The ultimate symbol of original sin. For the Fall was the loss of paradise: the loss of harmony, the loss of awareness of reality as it is. War thrusts us into a state of ultimate illusion, for it strikes out against what is the very heart of all that is real: namely, the oneness of all reality in God. War is the denial of the contemplative vision of reality. That is why contemplation is necessarily a rejection of all war.

Peace Movement and the Catholic Church

Will the Peace Movement in the Catholic Church continue to grow? I believe it will. As more and more people develop the contemplative side of their nature, as more and more people see the futility of war, there will be a stronger movement in the direction of non-violence and, as there was an emancipation proclamation against slavery a century ago, so there will be an emancipation proclamation against war.

Yet the Peace Movement is not yet at the center of Catholic moral teaching. For many it is still seen as very much of a minority position. As I wrote in *America* in 1993: The peace movement in the Roman Catholic Church today is in a situation similar to that of the liturgical movement in the decades before Vatican II. The liturgical movement comprised a zealous minority within the Church pushing for liturgical renewal; but the movement was outside the main line positions in the Catholic Church. The Second Vatican Council, with its sweeping liturgical reforms, changed all this: it placed the goals and directions of the liturgical movement at the heart of Catholic life and worship. In a somewhat similar way, the peace movement is a movement within the Church; and it is very much alive today. This by itself, however, does not make the Roman Catholic Church a "Christian Peace Church." That will happen only when the Church embraces the peace movement, places it at the center of her own life stream and thus makes it not just a movement in the Church but also a movement of the Church.

How Nonviolence Has Affected Me

One event that happened in my life that made the word "grace" seem more real to me than anything I had ever experienced before. It took place on October 23, 1983. It's a day I shall never forget. It was a Sunday and I had just finished presiding at a Eucharistic liturgy. As I was returning to my office, someone told me; "something terrible has just taken place; over 250 Marines were killed by a suicide terrorist attack in Beirut. My reaction was instantaneous. Strangely, it was not, first of all compassion or distress or anger. No, the thought that flashed into my mind seemed to have no connection whatsoever with the terrible massacre that had occurred. What came to my mind was; "I shall never smoke again." I had been a moderately heavy smoker and had smoked for over 40 years.

Why did that thought seem, for a brief time at least, to crowd out all other more appropriate reactions. I do not know. All I can surmise is that a process of intuition went on in my mind over which it seemed I had no control and to which I gave no direction. It was as if I was "reasoning" (though I went through no reasoning process at all): "this was a heinous act of violence. I went to make some immediate protest against this violence. There is one thing I can do immediately; I can cease doing the violence to my body that smoking involves. I shall never smoke again."

I am writing about this almost 30 years after the event. I have never smoked since that day nor have I had any desire to do so. And not even for a day did I experience any "withdrawal" symptoms, even though I had obviously had a strong addiction to tobacco. This may sound quite insignificant, and compared to the event that precipitated it, it certainly pales in importance. Yet, to this day I feel that this moment years ago was, as I have already said, one of the most palpable moments of grace that I have ever experienced.

    I cannot help but think that I was readied for this grace because of my commitment to contemplation and its sister nonviolence. My gratitude to Merton for pointing me in this direction.

Some examples of Cold War Letters:

To Etta Gullick:

> "...There is one task for me that takes precedence over everything else: working with such means as I have at my disposal for the abolition of war. This is like going into the prize ring blindfolded and with hands tied, since I am cloistered and subject to the most discouragingly long and frustrating kind of censorship on top of it. I must do what I can."(Cold War Letters, p.9)

To Jean Goss-Mayr

> "The great peril of the Cold War is the progressive deadening of conscience. This of course is s a process which was already well under way after World War I, and received a great impetus during the second war."(Cold War Letters, p, 48.)

To Sister Emmanuel

"...I think at least some contemplatives must try to understand the providential events of the day. God works in history, therefore a contemplative who has no sense of historical responsibility, is not a fully Christian contemplative: he is gazing at God as a static essence or as an intellectual light or as a nameless ground of being. But in reality we are face to face with the Lord of history and with Christ, the King and Savior, the Light of the world who comes forth from the Father and returns to the Father. We must comfort him in the awful paradoxes of our day, in which we see that our society is being judged....In a word we have to be Christians in all the full dimensions of the Gospel."

(Cold War Letters, p. 51

CHAPTER FOUR

MY CONVERSION TO
A NEW UNDERSTANDING OF CHURCH

The Church has always played a big role in my life. As a young boy, I served Mass every day in my parish Church. When I finished grade school, I entered the seminary. In 1943, I was ordained a priest of the Rochester diocese. I was like hundreds of young priests coming out of seminaries at a time when vocations were plentiful. What seminary taught us was that the Roman Catholic Church had, ready at hand, all the answers to all the questions of any importance that could ever come up. These answers were in our textbooks. Hence all we had to do was learn our textbooks. If we learned them well, we would be the most learned people in the community and would have all the answers that people would ever need. Moreover, the Catholic people, by and large, believed this too.

I want to take a moment to tell you what the church meant to us at this time. We knew that as a church we were on a journey. As we made this journey, we tended to identify the church with her institutional structure. The church was the pope pointing out to us, sometimes in his own writings sometimes through his delegates, bishops and priests the only way to make the journey and be sure of arriving at the desired end. He was the Holy Father. We were the children. And Father knew best.

The metaphor for the church of yesteryear was the pyramid. The pope was on the top with supreme power. Others below him, but still in the structure, acted as intermediaries to tell us what to do. And there were we, down at the bottom of the pyramid. Outside the institutional structure and grateful to it for so faithfully pointing out to us the way to go and furnishing us with the sacraments that helped us along the way. So when we spoke about the church (as for instance in asking the question; what does the church teach about such and such), we meant its institutional structure, of whom we were simply the grateful clients.

Now I would like to give a number of vignettes (experiences and events) that led to the gradual erosion of this very limited and limiting concept of the church.

1) **Discussion Group With Married Couples**

In the 40's and 50's I was moderator of a discussion group of about a dozen married couples. They met regularly every month. Many of them I saw through engagement to marriage, to lots of children and grandchildren. The meetings often went into the wee hours of the morning. I recall one incident in which one of the men came into the living room where we were meeting with his pajamas thrown over his shoulder and said to his wife; "Lucille, let us get to bed so that we can let these good people go home."

At these monthly meetings (I am almost ashamed to recall it), I was the oracle. No matter what the question was – morality, religious doctrines, politics, you name it – I was the person of final appeal. What I said was right. They were not sure that what they said was right, until I put the seal of my approval on it. [Well, maybe I am exaggerating a bit, but it did often seem that it was this way.]

This group continued to meet regularly for quite a number of years. But the group effectively died (in its original format, that is) some time in the 1950s. The reason: one couple made the decision that they could no longer accept the Church's teaching on birth control (a teaching that was so sternly set forth in *Casti Conubii*, the encyclical issued by Pope Pius XI in 1931). They had dared to question the Oracle and his papal mentor! They had dared to think for themselves! But I didn't dare to listen to them. Neither (I think, anyway) did other couples in the group. They felt sorry for this one couple who were obviously confused, because they had disagreed with the Oracle. At the time none of us could foresee that in 1968 Pope Paul VI in his encyclical, *Humanae Vitae*, would (more gently, but still firmly) reiterate the teaching of his predecessor. Much less could we have expected then that in 1969 I would publish my first book, entitled *The Lively Debate*, in which I would defend the right of Catholics to disagree with *Humanae Vitae*. Much had happened in the intervening years: I had come by this time to a whole new understanding of what we mean by Church.

2) The Liturgical Movement

In the 1940's and 50's I met regularly with several Rochester priests; Ed Lintz, Joe Cirincioni, Ben Ehman, to discuss the liturgical movement. It's a movement that began in Europe in Benedictine monasteries. It eventually came to the United States under the leadership of the Benedictine monastery at Collegeville, MN. The movement called for more active involvement by the people in the liturgy. It was a movement inspired by Pius X. In his 1903 Motu Proprio, Tra le Sollicitudini, he stated that "active participation in the liturgy is the primary and indispensible source of the true Christian spirit." Gradually in the United States the dialogue mass came into use, that is, a mass in which the people made responses to the priest. In 1938, Father Joseph F. Stedman, a priest of the diocese of

Brooklyn brought out a small missal with Latin and English facing one another. It made it very easy for people to follow the mass. In fact it was described as the, "you can't get lost missal." Gradually this missa recitata became widespread in the church. It prepared people for the liturgical reforms of Vatican II.

3) Reading Writers of Other Religions

Some time in the 1950s a group of priests of our Rochester diocese began to hold regular meetings in my office. We came together to read and discuss a number of well-known Protestant writers, such as Paul Tillich, John. A. T. Robinson, Harvey Cox and others (this was hardly something for Roman Catholic priests to do at that time). We came to realize that other Christian thinkers had things to share with us that could be valuable. This reading opened us to the desire for dialogue with representatives of other religions.

4) Catholic Action

In 1946 I was appointed to teach at Nazareth College. The 1950s were a time when Catholic Action had begun to play an important role for students on Catholic college campuses. It was Pope Pius XI who promoted Catholic Action and defined it as "the participation of the laity in the apostolate of the hierarchy." Groups were small: 8 to 10. Several such groups might be formed on one campus. (There were also Catholic actions groups for the working class, but I was not involved in them) The motto of the CA cells (as they were sometimes called) was: "Everything by the lay persons; nothing without the priest." This was the beginning of my realization of the importance of the laity in the apostolic work of the church.

5) Brazil

In 1982 I visited my friends, the Sisters of St. Joseph of Rochester, in Brazil. I arrived on New Year's Eve. The first Portuguese I learned was *"Feliz Ano Novo."* It was a handy line that got me through my entire visit. I was never lost for words. No matter what anyone asked of me, I simply said *"Feliz Ano Novo."* While in Brazil I had the opportunity of hearing about and visiting a number of base communities. In their meeting in Medellin, the Bishops described these communities as "the first and fundamental core of the church… the initial cell of the ecclesial structure, the focus for evangelization…" This was a never to be forgotten experience for me: coming to see the need for small groups of Christians to gather regularly to study the scriptures and make them become a dominant influence in their lives and their environment. This is a need I see as very important in the church today.

6) First English Mass

In October, 1964 it was my privilege to say the first English Mass in the diocese of Rochester. The reason for celebrating this Mass was to give the priests of the diocese some idea of what the "new" Mass would be like. As I look back it was a rather curious spectacle. The congregation was made up solely of priests. Since they had already said Mass in their parishes, I was the only one to receive communion. Still, it was a thrilling experience to be able for the first time to say Mass in our own language.

7) Lectures on Vatican II Documents

In the 1960s, Father Charles Curran and I were giving lectures on the various documents of Vatican II to the Sisters of St. Joseph who assembled in large numbers in Nazareth Academy's auditorium. The sisters were eager to know about these documents and they became effective instruments for getting the Council and its insights better known in the diocese. It was especially important that they were able to share their knowledge of these documents with students, laity and clergy. Church History

During my seminary days I had excellent courses in Church history. In 1949 I received a Master's degree in history at Canisius College in Buffalo, and in 1953, a Ph.D. from the University of Ottawa, also in history. My studies in history prepared me for the surprise announcement made on January 25, 1959 by Pope John XXIII that he was calling a council of the Catholic Church. Anyone fairly well acquainted with Church history will recall that Church councils have been fairly rare. Before John announced that he was calling a council, there had been in the 2000 years' story of the Church only twenty such gatherings. These councils met either to define Catholic teachings or to condemn propositions that were considered contrary to Christian faith. Two councils were held in the fourth century: the Council of Nicaea in 325 and the Council of Constantinople in 381. Two more were held in the fifth century; the Council of Ephesus in 431 and the Council of Chalcedon in 451. These councils defined Catholic teachings on the Incarnation and the Trinity. Other councils were held in later centuries, some of which were not of any great importance for the general church. The best remembered councils before Vatican II were the Council of Trent which met in stages from 1545-1563 (to deal with the issues raised by the Protestant Reformation) and the Council of Vatican I (to deal with issues of modernity) in 1869-1870. Then in 1959, Pope John XXIII surprised the world by announcing that a Council of the church would be held.

These vignettes (events, experiences) helped me to understand the Second Vatican Council and the new meaning of church that it gave us

A Brief History of the Second Vatican Council

The four years of this Council – 1962 to 1965 – witnessed a development in the life of the Catholic Church unparalleled in modern history. The Council was a response to the call of Pope John XXIII for *aggiornamento*, an updating of the Church that would make the Gospel of Jesus Christ once again an influential force in a world that seemed to be leaving it behind. John XXIII was elected pope October 28, 1958. It was a tumultuous time in both the Church and the world. Three years before his election, Rosa Parks on December 1, 1955, made her brave refusal that led to the Montgomery bus boycott and subsequent civil rights' legislation in the United States. This was the time of the Cold War between the two superpowers: Russia and the United States. American forces were bogged down in Viet Nam. Peace activists were becoming more numerous and more vocal in protesting war and violence.

One day, not long after his election as pope, John XXIII was discussing with Cardinal Tardini, his secretary of state, the troubled condition of the world. Suddenly an inspiration came to him: "Un concilio!" Tardini was enthusiastic: "Si! Si! Un concilio!" The Pope announced his intention to call a council to a number of cardinals at a gathering of a small number of them in the church of St. Paul outside the walls. The Roman curia did not share the pope's enthusiasm. They saw a council as a mistake. They knew how to run the Church. Unable to dissuade the pope, they gave passive acquiescence with the hope that they could control the council. They were especially fearful of movements stirring in the north: France, Germany, Holland, Belgium, Austria. Their fears were well captured in the title of a book on the Council by Ralph Wiltgen, called *The Rhine Flows into the Tiber*. They suspected that the new reformers in the Church seemed to be wanting what Luther and other reformers had wanted in 16th century: vernacular liturgy, biblical studies by lay people, restructuring of the Curia, a more collegial approach to authority. All this had been settled 400 years ago! So they thought!

    Unable to dissuade the Pope from having the Council, the curial officials were determined to control it. Their intent was to get the Council over as quickly as possible so that they could go back to running things as usual. In the very first weeks the Bishops, especially those the Curia most feared, made clear that they had different ideas. They had brought their theologians with them and the theologians led discussions with the bishops – discussions that educated the bishops and helped them in writing the Council documents. These theologians included people like Congar, Chenu, Rahner and deLubac (to mention just a few). They also included a young theologian named Joseph Ratzinger.

On December 25, 1961 Pope John signed the bull formally convoking the Council. Pope John XXIII in his opening address on October 11, 1962, set the tone for the council. He spoke of the Church bringing herself up to date (aggiornamento). He warned against those persons who look at the world and see nothing but prevarication and ruin. "We feel we must disagree with those prophets of gloom, who are always forecasting disaster. In the present order of things, divine Providence is leading us to a ***new order of human relations*** ….directed toward the fulfillment of God's superior and inscrutable designs." The pope made clear that the Church may never depart from the sacred patrimony of truth received from the Fathers. Still, he pointed out "the substance of the ancient doctrine is one thing, and the way in which it is presented is another." It is the latter that must be given great consideration in a way that is pastoral in character. The Church must always oppose errors. But nowadays, the Pope insisted, the Church prefers to make use of the medicine of mercy rather than that of severity.

"The Council, now beginning, rises in the Church like daybreak, a forerunner of most splendid light. **But it is now only dawn.**"

The World Scene

As the Council Fathers gathered, there was anything but dawn in the world outside, specifically an ominous Cold War confrontation between Russia and the United States seemed to be imminent. Nikita Khrushchev had agreed to send nuclear weapons to Cuba. Ships bearing them were on the way. President John F. Kennedy threatened retaliation. The possibility of a deadly nuclear war threatened the peace of the world. Khrushchev decided he should withdraw his threat, but needed a way out. Through an intermediary he contacted Pope John XXIII telling him that a message from him might avert the danger that threatened. On October 24, 1962, Pope John issued a strong statement responding to Khrushchev: "We beg all governments not to remain deaf to the cry of humanity. That they do all that is in their power to save peace." The next day on the front page of Pravda, the official mouthpiece of the Soviet Communist party, carried the Pope's message, with the title: "We beg all governments not to remain deaf to this cry of humanity that they do all in their power to save peace." Khrushchev listened and October 28, the Soviet ships turned around and returned home. Through the Pope's intervention the scourge of a nuclear war may have been averted.

Meanwhile Back at the First Session of the Council

The first session began on October 11, 1962 and ended on December 8, 1962. October 13, 1962, marked the initial working session of the Council. The first item on the agenda was to elect members for the ten conciliar commissions. Each would have 16 elected and 18 appointed members. Cardinal Ottaviani had prepared a list of 160 names with curia members heavily represented. Cardinal Accille Lienart addressed the Council and made the point that the Bishops did not know one another and needed time to get acquainted. He asked, therefore, that the vote be postponed so that the Bishops could draw up their own list. His proposal was accepted and the vote was postponed. In the voting for the various documents the bishops signed a paper on which they could vote in three possible ways. 1) *placet* (accept) or 2) *non placet* (reject) or 3) *placet juxta modum* (accept with reservations). On October 16, a new slate of commission members was presented and approved. This was the beginning of the bishops' struggle against curial intransigence .It is interesting to mention that there were coffee shops set up on the side aisles of St. Peter's Basilica to accommodate the almost three-thousand persons gathered each day for the Council's sessions. These coffee shops were given the name "Bar-Jonah" (Hebrew for 'Son of John'), a scriptural reference to St. Peter. These offered the bishops and their theologians a place to discuss what was going on in the Council. It was Pope John who decided that these coffee shops be set up. He is reported as having said that if the bishops didn't have a place to smoke their cigarettes, they would be puffing them under their miters.

      Seven schemas (documents) were presented to the Bishops. The document on Liturgy received general approval at the first session though it would not be promulgated until the next session. The document on Revelation in the form in which it was presented was roundly rejected. On November 26, the document on the Church was presented. It was also strongly criticized. Cardinal Josef De Smedt, Bishop of Bruges, delivered one of the most famous and oft-quoted speeches of the Council denouncing the document for triumphalism, clericalism and juridicism. It presented the Church as a pyramidal structure with all power flowing from the top to the bottom. The reality of the People of God is more fundamental in the Church, he maintained, than a hierarchy. "We must be aware of falling into some kind of bishop-worship or pope-worship." The Church, he said, is more our mother than a juridical institution. (See John O'Malley: ***What Happened at Vatican II***, pg 155.)During the intersession Cardinal Suenens' proposed a distinction between the Church looking inward (for her own identity) and looking outward (for her relation to and responsibility for the world). This out looking toward the world as something to embrace rather than to condemn set a whole new direction that had never been part of earlier councils. As I said in an article that appeared in a St. Anthony Messenger magazine "the council looked upon the world and smiled instead of frowning." Thus it became clear that before the first session ended the Council fathers had rejected the documents given to them beforehand and had called for a rewriting. Pope John XXIII concurred and ordered the drafting of new documents. Thus, though no documents were promulgated at the first session, much had been accomplished. The lines had been drawn and the divisions between the ***progressive majority*** and the ***hold-the-line minority*** were clear.

From my diocese Bishop Kearney and auxiliary Bishop Casey arrived in Rome for the first session of the Council. Bishop Kearney never caught on to the spirit of what was happening at the Council and did not return for the remaining sessions. Bishop Casey, on the other hand, was profoundly influenced and was very much present at all the remaining sessions. Sr. Anne Mary Dooley, a Sister of Saint Joseph of Rochester, NY, was at the press office in

Rome and had frequent contact with Bishop Casey and other bishops and theologians at the Council.

The Death of a Pope

Pope John XXIII died on June 3, 1963 – after a long and painful illness in which he offered his sufferings for the success of the Council. On June 21, Giovanni Battista Montini, the cardinal of Milan, was elected to succeed him and took the name Paul VI. For the remaining three sessions, therefore, the Council became that of Paul VI. His sympathies were with the progressive majority, but he had himself been a member of the Curia and at times yielded to pressure from some of the curial hard-liners.

During the intersession, the documents had been reworked. These new versions were presented to the bishops at the second session of the Council. Perhaps most significant was the suggestion that in the document on the Church, the Chapter on the People of God should become Chapter 2 and thus be placed before the Chapter on the Hierarchy. When a Pope dies, a Council is automatically dissolved. Pope Paul, immediately upon his election announced that the Council would continue.

The Second Session of the Council

Pope Paul opened the Council on September 29, 1963 with an address in which he stressed the pastoral nature of the council and emphasized the following purposes:

- to more define more fully the nature of the church and the role of the bishop;
- to renew the church;

- to restore the unity among all Christians, including a seeking of pardon for Catholic contributions to separation; and to start a dialogue with the contemporary world.

At the second session (1963) several documents were discussed: on Revelation, on the Church and on Liturgy. The last, The Constitution on the Sacred Liturgy was approved by a large vote of the majority. It was a document that transformed our thinking about liturgy. The document stated "the Liturgy is the summit toward which the activity of the Church is directed; it is also the source from which all its powers flow." The way toward this document had been prepared for by the liturgical movement that began many years earlier.

Most significant changes were made in the document on the Church. Chapter 1, which in the earlier draft had been called "The Church Militant," became "The Church as Mystery." This shows the recovery of the spiritual dimension of the Church. A new Chapter was added: Chapter 4 entitled "The Universal Call to Holiness." The doctrine of collegiality came in for much discussion. It was made clear that the bishops are vicars of Christ and are not to be thought of as vicars of the Roman pontiff. They exercise an authority that is properly their own and really govern the flocks that are theirs. On September 30, Giuseppe Gargitter, Bishop of Bolzano-Bressone, proposed that there be a new Chapter 2 on the "People of God" that would precede the Chapter on the "Hierarchy." This had been suggested by Cardinal Suenens during the intercession. (as I mentioned earlier)

The Council debated whether it is only the Roman Catholic Church that is the true Church of Christ stating that the Church of Christ is (*est*) the Roman Catholic Church. Many bishops found this objectionable as it implied that Orthodox and Protestant churches are not churches in any real sense. The document was changed and the Latin *est* was replaced with "*subsisted in*." This means that the Church of Christ is not identical with the Catholic church. The Church of Christ "subsists in", that is, exists or lives in the Catholic church, but not exclusively there. Elements of truth and sanctification are found in non-Catholic Christian communities as well. The ecumenical implications of this tentative opening are enormous. (See Edward P. Hahnenberg, *The Concise Guide to the Documents of Vatican II*, pg. 42.)

Two documents were promulgated at the second session: the one on Liturgy and the one on Social Communication.

The Third Session of the Council

At the second session Cardinal Suenens noted that there were no women represented at the Council, yet, "if I am not mistaken," he said, "they represent half of the human race." Fifteen women observers were invited to the Third Session. Among the 15 women was Sister Mary Luke Tobin, a sister of Loretto who represented American women religious. Sister Mary Luke commented, "15 compared to more than 2,000 is hardly a quota but it is a start." During this period, which began on the 14th of September, 1964, a number of schema were discussed. Only three documents were promulgated: the Church (*Lumen Gentium*) Catholic Eastern Churches and

Ecumenism. At the third session the document on the Church, which had gone through long and often acrimonious discussion, was promulgated. Many other things of importance happened during the third session. The famous schema 13, which eventually became ***The Pastoral Constitution on the Church in the Modern World***, was introduced, as well as the Declaration on Religious Freedom and the declaration on the Jews. The first was strongly debated. To the dismay of many, the declaration on the Jews was voted down. It had been a superb statement. One of the reasons that it was rejected was the opposition of Catholic bishops in Arab countries who felt the document might give the impression that the Church was recognizing the state of Israel. Recall this was 1964 three years before the 1967 six-day war that considerably expanded Jewish territory. It was a time when Arabs refused to accept the very existence of Israel as a state.

  Jewish leaders were bitterly upset by the rejection of the declaration on the Jews, especially after the rumor spread that in the next session a new document which expressed the "Church's desire and expectation of the union of the Church with the Jewish people." The well known Jewish scholar and writer, Abraham Joshua Heschel wrote to Thomas Merton about his anguish and visited him at Gethsemani. He told Merton that he had repeatedly said to the leaders at the Vatican and in particular to Pope Paul VI: "I am ready to go to Auschwitz any time, if faced with the alternative of conversion or death." That very day Merton wrote to Cardinal Bea. Among other things, in a memorable letter he said: "I am personally convinced that the grace to truly see the Church in her humility and in her splendor may perhaps not be granted to the Council Fathers, if they fail to take account of her relation to the anguished Synagogue…If she forgoes this opportunity out of temporal and political motives…will she not by that very fact manifest that she has in some way forgotten her own true identity. Is not the whole meaning and purpose of the Council at stake?" (HGL, 433)

The Fourth Session of the Council

The fourth session began on September 14 and ended on December 8, 1965. Eleven documents remained to be put in final form.**Dei Verbum-** At this fourth session the council after much discussion made clear that there are not two sources of revelation (scripture and tradition) but one revelation namely the revelation of Jesus Christ. In the document on revelation the council sought to revive the central role of scripture in the theological and devotional life of the church, building upon the work of earlier popes encrafting a modern approach to scriptural analysis and interpretation. The church was to continue to provide versions of the bible in the "Mother tongues" of the faithful, and both clergy and laity were to continue to make bible study a central part of their lives. This affirmed the importance of Sacred Scripture as attested by *Providentissimus Deus* by Pope Leo XIII and the writings of the saints and popes throughout history. It also approved historical and critical interpretations of scripture as made clear in Pius XII, 1943 encyclical, *Divino Afflante Spiritu.***Nostra Aetate -** Happily, in the Fourth Session, the Council Fathers did produce a quite satisfactory document on non-Christian religions, ***Nostra Aetate***. The section in this document on Judaism is quite good and acceptable. In fact it would have been hailed as a remarkable document, were it not for the fact that it replaced an earlier document that had been even better, namely the original one that the previous session of the Council had rejected. **Dignitatis Humanae** - This was one of the more controversial documents that was approved. It is in marked contrast with the Syllabus of Errors. This document approved by Pope Pius IX in 1864 insisted on state establishment of the Catholic religion and condemned those who denied that the Catholic religion should be treated as the only religion of the state, and that all other forms of worship whatever should be excluded. Significantly one hundred years later – between 1963 and 1965 – a very different approach to the relationship of Church and state was being discussed at the Second Vatican Council: an approach that blossomed into ***The Declaration on Religious Freedom***. (*Dignitatis Humanae*) This document was at first an appendix to the document on Ecumenism, but later received its own independent status.

There were those at the Council who continued to hold the position set forth by Pius IX at Vatican I. They based their reasoning on the belief that the Catholic religion was the one true religion and therefore should be established by the state and that other religions should not be allowed. If Catholics were not in a majority in a country other religions should, at most, be tolerated. Fundamental to their thinking was also the position that "error has no rights."

John Courtney Murray (1904-1967), an American Jesuit theologian was the principal architect of ***The***

Declaration on Religious Freedom. In the decades preceding the Council, Murray had written extensively on the relationship of the religious pluralism accepted in the American political tradition and the Roman Catholic claim to possess the truths necessary for salvation and equally necessary for the proper ordering of society. Murray had not been invited to the first session of the Council, but in 1963 he accompanied Cardinal Spellman of New York who managed to get him accepted as a *peritus* on Cardinal Bea's Secretariat for Christian Unity.

The *Declaration* states that the human person has a right to religious freedom. A right rooted in "the dignity of the human person as this is known from the revealed word of God and from reason itself."(2) Religious freedom means (a) that all people enjoy immunity from coercion by any human power, (b) that no one should be forced to act against his (her) conscience nor (c) prevented from acting according to his (her) conscience.

Pope Paul VI called this *Declaration,* accepted by the Council on December 7, 1965, "one of the major texts of the Council." On December 7, 1965, the final day of the Second Vatican Council, the council fathers adopted the much discussed *The Pastoral Constitution on the Church in the Modern World.(Gaudium et spes)* Its tone and direction differed significantly from the other major documents of Vatican II. In other important documents the Church turned inward to shed the light of the Gospel on herself to see what God willed her to be. In this document, the Church looked outward to discover in the light of the Gospel her role in today's world: a world of which she is after all a part, but a world that in many ways had ceased to take her seriously.

The Church not only looked outward; it did so in a way that no previous Church council had ever done. It looked at the world and it "smiled," somewhat as God must have smiled when God gazed on the world He had created and "saw that it was very good." Other councils, by contrast, had looked at the world and ignored it or deplored it, seeing it as a place of sin and corruption that they felt compelled to condemn. Vatican II abandoned this mentality: it took the world to its heart in a spirit of concern and compassion. It would partner with the world in discerning "the true signs of God's presence and purpose in the events, needs and desires, which it shares with the rest of today's women and men" (11).

A persistently positive attitude toward that world and an earnest desire to enter into dialogue with it make this document unique in the history of council documents. Its thrust is essentially incarnational. The incarnation means that Christ did not redeem the world from afar, but by becoming involved in the human situation. This incarnational principle was adopted by the Council and gave birth to a new understanding of the Church's mission. Before the Council her mission was envisioned primarily as other-world directed, namely, focused almost exclusively on enabling individuals to attain eternal salvation. *Gaudium et Spes* moved Catholics toward a new way of thinking that saw the Church's mission as witnessing also to the love and compassion of God in the here and now. Divine love and compassion call us to work for justice, peace, and healing in our global world.

Thus it was that on the last day of the formal meetings of the Council, on December 7, 1965, eleven documents were promulgated. Two truly important documents promulgated were **Declaration on Religious Freedom (*Dignitatis Humanae*)** and the **Pastoral Constitution on the Church in the Modern World (*Gaudium et Spes*)** The following day, December 8, 1965, Pope Paul VI presided at a solemn Mass in the piazza of St. Peter's. Sister Anne Mary Dooley, together with Sister Florian Reichart (Sisters of St. Joseph of Rochester) were privileged to be at both the last formal meeting of the Council (on December 7) and also at the mass on December 8, closing the council. Sister Anne Mary wrote a moving letter to Mother Agnes Cecilia and the Sisters of St. Joseph describing these two events.

A List of the Sixteen Documents Promulgated by Vatican II

Of the sixteen only four were given the name of Constitution. Nine of the other twelve documents were called decrees: the remaining three were designated as Declarations. The four Constitutions should be given primary importance. They are concerned with those matters that are constitutive of Catholic faith. They treat substantive doctrinal issues that pertain to the very nature of the church. The decrees and declarations have as their primary intent to offer directions for action in various areas. We might say, therefore that the constitutions stand on their own in the way that the decrees and declarations do not. It might be put this way if the council had issued no decrees and declarations in all we might presumably be able to construct the basic direction they suggest from the content on the constitutions. The converse would not be true, that is if we had only the decrees and declarations it would be much more difficult to reconstruct from them the content of the constitutions.

The four constitutions are:

1. The Dogmatic Constitution on Divine Revelation (Dei Verbum)
2. The Dogmatic Constitution on the Church (Lumen Gentium)
3. The Constitution on the Sacred Liturgy (Sacrosanctum Concilium)
4. The Pastoral Constitution on the Church in the Modern World (Gaudium et Spes)

Some Important Decrees

1. Decree on the Pastoral Office of Bishops in the Church (*Christus Dominus*)
2. Decree Upon Renewal of Religious Life (*Perfectae Caritatis*)
3. Decree on the Apostolate of Lay People (*Apostolicam Actuositatem*)
4. Decree on Ecumenism (*Unitatis Redintegratio*)

Two Important Declarations

1. Declaration on Religious Liberty (*Dignitatis Humanae*)
2. Declaration on the Relationship of the Church to Non-Christian Religions *(Nostra Aetate)*

My Reflections

What we have written about thus far is a brief story of the Second Vatican Council and what it hoped to accomplish. Now almost 50 years removed from the council we need to evaluate what has happened to the church in these intervening years. In his opening address to the Council, Pope John XXIII said that at the time it was only dawn. Has the daylight come? Has the vision of Vatican II been realized in the church? Surely much has been accomplished in which we can take great joy. We have come a long way. But sad to say I feel that the church seems to have fallen on evil times. Excitement seems to have gone out of the life of the church: the excitement we experienced during the time of the council and in my own Diocese of Rochester the excitement engendered by our diocesan synod held in the 1980's. Today the steps being taken to recentralize the church have taken a lot of the joy out of the church for those who really love the church and believe it is their church. And it feels almost as if it is being taken away from them. Still we are God's people on pilgrimage toward the fullness of the kingdom. Can the spark ignited by Vatican II be re-enkindled for a new generation of disciples of Jesus? Can we make the optimism of the Gospel relevant once again? Can we hope that the Holy Spirit who inspired the calling of the Council will move the whole people of God (laity, religious, priests, bishops) to build the Church of a blessed future -- and build it on all that has already been accomplished through the Council? The future belongs to us – God's pilgrim people. We must build that future. We must have the courage to hope.

A Preliminary Reflection

You will remember that in Chapter One, I discussed two models of the church that emerged from comparing the

Gospel of Matthew with the Gospel of John. They presented two models of the church; one in which the Holy Spirit operates in the church's leadership (Matthew's Gospel), the other in which the spirit operates in all of the disciples of Jesus. These are certainly different ways of understanding the church. But they are not mutually exclusive they are meant to be complimentary. The leadership model assures us that there is someone, first in the local church (the Bishop), then among all the local bishops (the Bishop of Rome) who, after all the dialogue has taken place is able finally to say in the name of all: "This is the faith of the church. This is what we believe." Unless we are content to see the church as a kind of endless debating society, where nothing is ever definite, we very much need this kind of leadership.On the other hand the "Paraclete" model, in which the spirit operates in all the members, helps to insure a vitality, a creativity, a flexibility, as the spirit operates among many people to deepen our understanding of who Jesus is and who we are as his disciples.For the good of the church we need both models. The complimentarity of the two models works most smoothly when there is deep mutual respect between the hierarchal authority and the other baptized members of the church, when one is not seen as a threat to the other. Such mutuality is not easy to achieve and we seem to be living at a time when a marriage of the two appears almost as if on the verge of a divorce.

    I recall the story of a young woman who was beautiful but not very intelligent. who suggested to George Bernard Shaw "why don't we marry? Just think of a child with my looks and your brain." Shaw replied, "there is another possibility, a child with your brain and my looks."

Matthean Influence
The Assent of the Faithful
to the Teaching of the Magisterium

For much of the Twentieth Century the church has operated out of a Matthean understanding of the church. Vatican II was an attempt - not completely successful - of adding a Johannine understanding of church. What is needed today is the injection of a strong dose of Johanine thinking into the ecclesial mix. We cannot absolutize the role of the hierarchy, important as it is. At the same time neither can we absolutize the sense of the faithful. We need to realize that both stirrings of the Spirit in the Church are important. We do not harmonize them by suppressing one or other. Our only viable choice is to live with the tensions that such stirrings of the Spirit may create at a given time in our history.

It is important that we have a clear understanding of Matthean ecclesiology. Vatican II has helped. The Council has made clear (well, sort of) the approach we need to take to the teachings of the hierarchical magisterium. We are called in article 25 of Lumen Gentium to accept "with submission of will and mind" the authentic teachings of the Roman Pontiff and also the bishops teaching in union with him. "Submission" in the phrase "submission of mind and will" is, in the Latin text of Vatican II *obsequium religiosum*". The meaning of this phrase has been much debated. "Submission "is a strong translation of it; "respect" would be a weak translation. Richard McCormick has suggested the following: "a docile personal attempt to assimilate the teaching," In the context in which he is writing he adds that this attempt may end in the inability to assimilate. This inability to assimilate a magisterial teaching forces a person, who wants to be honest to his or her conscience, to dissent from such teaching.

Dissent: Is It Ever Permissible?

Dissent, so it seems to me, ought to be a very rare experience in the life of the Church. It would be rare, I believe, if Johannine ecclesiology were taken more seriously. Dissent would be rare, if we had a clearer understanding of the attitude which the magisterium in the Church ought to take toward that other "stirring of the Spirit" which also operates in the Church. The laity must give "*obseqium religiosum"* to the teachings of the magisterium. Yes, of course. But what kind of attention ought the magisterium to give to the stirrings of the Spirit in God's holy people? (By God's holy people I mean to include diocesan priests and deacons as well as the rest of the baptized.) This is an ecclesial question that has not yet been adequately addressed. Over a century and a quarter ago, John Henry Newman tried to address it in an article in the Catholic periodical, *The Rambler*. His article "On Consulting the Faithful in Matters of Doctrine" was not well received in his day. It was an idea whose time had not yet come.

I think it is fair to say that its time came at Vatican II. The earliest documents given to the bishops when they arrived for the Council were written by Curial officials and they clearly embodied a Matthean understanding of the Church. The majority of the bishops did their best to modify these documents by introducing into them elements of Johannine thinking.

It should be clear that, if we accept the Johannine ecclesiology, then failure on the part of church authority to listen to the *sensus fidelium* could well amount to a refusal to hear what the Spirit truly is saying to the church, but in a way other than through magisterial teaching. Hearing the voice of concerned and committed laity is important for the life and health of the church. A bishop once asked Newman, in a rather disparaging tone of voice: "who are the laity, anyway?" Newman replied: "The Church would look foolish without them."

Johannine Influence
The Listening of the Hierarchy
to the Voice of the People of God

A while ago I was invited to give a talk to the Pastoral Associates of our diocese on the topic: "The Church of the Third Millennium." I'm not sure if I am going to see any of it, but I did take a shot at the topic. The tenor of my talk was that the first millennium was the millennium of the bishops, the second millennium that of the monarchical papacy. The third millennium I predicted would be that of the baptized. If the catch phrase for the first millennium was: "Where the bishop is, there is the church," and for the second millennium: "Where Peter is, there is the church," for the third millennium it will be: "Where the people are, there is the church."

Or to put it in terms of the theme of this chapter, the third millennium will witness a healthy infusion of Johannine ecclesiology into the church's life and activity. Not to override the Matthean ecclesiology (which must always be there), but to inject a new source of life into it. For we (who live in the local Church of Rochester, New York) do not belong to Bishop Clark's church; Bishop Clark belongs to our church. We do not belong to Pope Benedict's church; Pope Benedict belongs to our church. By this I simply mean that the only claim that Bishop Clark and Pope Benedict XVI have to belong to the church of Jesus Christ is the same claim that each of us has: namely, they and we were all baptized into Christ's church.

One of the questions the third millennium must face is: how can we get the voice of God's people heard in the church? Vatican II tried to address this issue. In article 12, it says: "The body of the faithful as a whole, who have received the anointing of the holy one, cannot err in matters of belief." The Council Fathers at this point quote Johannine ecclesiology, calling attention to the first epistle of John, chapter 2, verses 20 and 27.

Verse 20 says: "You have the anointing that comes from the Holy One, so that all knowledge is yours," Verse 27 is even stronger: "As for you the anointing you have received from him remains in your hearts. This means you have no need for anyone to teach you. Rather as his anointing teaches you about all things and is true --free from any lie-- remain in him as that anointing taught you." That's a rather hearty dose of Johannine ecclesiology, even for Vatican II!But ultimately there is a failure of nerve on the part of the Council Fathers. After speaking of the insights that this *sensus fidelium* can bring into the life of the church, it goes on to say: "All this it does under the lead of the sacred teaching authority, to which it loyally defers."

Well, yes. Most of the time. But what if what the Spirit seems to be saying through the faithful is not in agreement with what hierarchy is saying? Does that automatically make it wrong? If it does, then we are in effect saying there is but a single stirring of the Spirit in the Church to which everything else that seems to be a stirring of the Spirit must yield. Or, to put this another way, must we say that the stirring of the Spirit among the people of God doesn't really count unless and until it has the approval of the hierarchy? This would be the triumph of what I have called Matthean ecclesiology.

Getting The Voice Of The People Heard

So I return to what I think is the most important ecclesiological question that must be faced in the Third Millennium: How can we get the voice of God's people heard in the church? One of the things I think needs to happen is a change in attitude on the part of the magisterium, most particularly the Roman Magisterium. They must move away from the position that they are expected to have all the answers -- to an attitude of listening to public opinion in the church. In 1959 (before the Council was convened) Karl Rahner wrote that church leaders need human help as well as divine. In his book *Free Speech in the Church* he says: Public opinion is one of the means whereby the Church's official leaders, who need human help as well as divine, get to know something about the actual situation within which and taking account of which, they are to lead and guide the people. They need to know how people are thinking and feeling, what they have set their hearts and wishes on, what their problem are, what they find difficult, in what respects their feelings have changed, where they find the traditional answers or rulings insufficient, what they would like to see changed...and so on.

This, of course, will make unaccustomed demands on church leaders, in the way of patience and a greater openness to dialogue. It will also call them to an admission of a certain degree of uncertainty on some issues and a willingness to wait for time and dialogue to bring greater clarity. It will mean that church teaching and policy will be less assured that it always has the right position. This will call for a greater flexibility and a more hospitable openness to change than has been true in the past.

Another way of reflecting on the creative tensions that help the church to continue to be faithful and continue to grow is to remember the two Saints who are honored in connection with Rome, namely Saints Peter and Paul. Perhaps one way of understanding the relationship of Peter and Paul is to reflect on the metaphors that can be applied to each of them. Thus Peter (Matthew 16:18) is the "Rock". He stands for stability and for preservation of the heritage of faith handed down to us. Paul, (Philippians 12:16) on the other hand, is the "Runner', who is the innovator. He wants to probe that heritage and see what new insights it can offer. Peter and Paul, we may say, represent two different but not necessarily conflicting- thrusts in the church; Peter the thrust from the center for the unity in love of the local churches, Paul, the thrust for the uniqueness of the local churches. These two thrusts "the one for unity among the churches, the other for the uniqueness of the local churches" by their very nature create a certain tension. This tension can be healthy as long as it creative.

Unity of the church is essential, but it is not the same as universality. It is Paul who stands as a guardian against a forced uniformity. Concern for essential unity among the churches and respect for the uniqueness of the local churches are both necessary for the church to be faithful to the Gospel.

Throughout history there have been periods wherein--to the detriment of the church-- one or other of these thrusts has became predominate. For example, in the period following Vatican I- "a period stretching from 1870 and reaching well into the first part of the twentieth century"- witnessed a fierce emphasis on uniformity that brought Catholic scholarship practically to a stand still. To say anything innovative was to court the charge of heresy. There is much in that history of which we cannot be proud. Someone wrote about the period "Rome lauds those who obey her because they do not care; she punishes those who disagree with her because they care."

The second Vatican Council tried to coordinate collegiality "which recognizes unique importance of each local church" with the primacy of the Bishop of Rome. This was an effort to balance, not eliminate the two different thrusts in the church. The Council tried to preserve a creative tension between stability and openness. Thus, it made clear the fundamental Catholic truth; that the bishops of local churches are "vicars of Christ" in that local church. At the same time it recognized the importance of the office of the Pope who is at the center and who is rightly concerned with the unity of the church.

In the euphoric years immediately following the council, their efforts seemed to have been succeeding.

There was new respect for the local churches. There was a new invitation to the laity to become involved in the affairs of the local church. There was a realization that the total realty of church is experienced in the local church. Yet the local church does not exist in isolation from other local churches. That is why the Church of Rome is so necessary. More and more we have come to understand the importance of preserving a delicate balance between unity and openness, if we are to remain faithful to the Stirrings of the Spirit in both the local church and that particular local church "the Church of Rome" that is at the center of Catholic unity. It was heartening to hear Pope Benedict XVI say that the quest for full visible Christian unity would be the "primary commitment" of his Pontificate, calling it "His ambition and compelling duty." We can only pray that the Holy Spirit who guides the church will enable us to achieve that delicate balance of stability and openness that will best serve the Gospel of Jesus Christ.

More Specific Reflections

1. Clarifying Our Understanding of the People of God

Yves Congar once remarked that it was not the laity who had to clarify their relationship to the hierarchy: rather it was the hierarchy that had to clarify its relationship to the laity. There is a sense in which all members of the church belong to the laity. For the word "laity" comes from the Greek word *Laos*, a word that simply means people. First and foremost, therefore laity (*laos*) really includes popes, bishops, priests, all God's people. At the opening of the second session of the council a memorial Mass was celebrated by the Council Fathers for Pope John XXIII.

Cardinal Suenens delivered the homily. In the course of his tribute to Pope John the Cardinal said: "The greatest day in the life of Pope John was not the day he became pope or the day he was ordained a bishop; neither was it the day he was ordained a priest. The greatest day in the life of Pope John was the day on which he was baptized into Christ."

I remember some time ago a young priest came to see me. It was soon after Pope John Paul II had issued **Ordinatio Sacerdotalis,** his document of the non-ordinabilty of women. The priest was terribly upset, not primarily because of the conclusion that the Pope drew (though that was certainly part of his concern) but principally because the Pope ordered that all discussion of the issue of the ordination of women was to stop. This my friend saw as unpardonable. "The document" he said, "Imposes; it does not persuade." It scarcely makes any effort to persuade. It simply says that we have to stop thinking and [he said] "This I simply cannot do". There wasn't a great deal I could say to him except that I had the same problems as he had. I just wasn't as disturbed about this document as he was. We talked for a long time.

One of the things I said to him that seemed to help a bit was this. I said: "Remember, you do not belong to the Pope's Church. The Pope belongs to our Church. His claim to membership in the Church of Christ is exactly the same as yours and mine and every other Christian. He belongs to the Church, not because he is Pope or bishop or priest, but because, like you and me, he was baptized into Jesus Christ." I told him the story of the memorial Mass celebrated by the Council Fathers for Pope John XXIII and the homily given by Cardinal Suenens.

It could well be said that this concept of the importance of baptism sums up a fundamental emphasis of the Council and helps us understand why the Church of Rochester back in the early 80's had a diocesan Synod. The Church must not be seen as divided into clergy and laity, with the clergy always in the posts of command. The Church is the communion of those who have been baptized into Christ Jesus. Ministry whether lay or ordained, far from separating ministers from the rest of the baptized, calls them to the service of their sisters and brothers. The Second Vatican Council says that, just as the laity have Christ for their brother, who became servant of all, so they have for their brothers those in the sacred ministry, (L.G., art. 32)This is why I stressed for my priest-friend that "it isn't the Pope's Church. It is our Church." I realized, though, that that was not an adequate response. In a sense it made the problem more severe. For I sensed that he felt: "If it's our Church, then why aren't we consulted? Why aren't we listened to?" This priest was not a way-out radical. He was a good, honest priest trying to be a pastoral priest and finding certain institutional aspects of the Church obstructing rather than assisting his ministry. It was not that he rejected authority in the Church. He objected to the way in which it was being exercised. He understood that the Church was not a democracy, but he did not see why more democratic procedures could not be followed in the Church's understanding and articulation of the Christian reality. And he is by no means the only one who feels that way.

The Second Vatican Council also emphasizes the importance of baptism when it speaks of the "apostolate of the laity." That apostolate is no longer described as it was in the past. Those of you who may have been involved in Catholic Action in the 1940s and '50s will remember the well known definition of Catholic Action given by Pius XI: "the participation of the laity in the apostolate of the hierarchy." The apostolate, the mission, of the Church belonged to the hierarchy. Through Catholic Action the laity were allowed to participate in that mission; but it was clearly understood that the mission belonged to the hierarchy. Vatican II changed this. It speaks of the role of the laity as" a participation in the saving mission of the Church itself." "Through their baptism and confirmation all are commissioned to that apostolate by the Lord Himself." (art.33)

Besides its emphasis on the importance of baptism and the role of the people of God, the Second Vatican Council also attempted to decentralize the Church. It did this by emphasizing the importance of the local Church. It is in the local Church --in the Church of Rochester or Syracuse or whatever local Church you belong to-- that you and I experience the reality of being Church.

There is a story about a World War I chaplain, Father Frank Duffy, that is pertinent here. He is well known as the chaplain of the Fighting 69th Division and there is a statue in his honor at Duffy Square between 46 and 47th Street in New York City. One day on the battlefield a solder approached him. The soldier knew that he was a chaplain, but did not know the Church he belonged to. So he asked: "Are you a Roman Catholic?" Father Duffy paused for a moment and then answered: "Well, actually,

I'm a New York Catholic." His answer embodied an excellent theology of the Church.

What he was saying is that he was a Catholic because he belonged to the local Catholic Church of New York. You and I could well say of ourselves something similar to what he said. If any one of us were asked: "Are you a Roman Catholic?" we could in all truth say: "Well, actually, I'm a Rochester (or Syracuse, etc.) Catholic."

In the strictest sense of the term a Roman Catholic is a Catholic who lives in Rome, Italy. If you were to go to Rome, Italy and ask a person there: "Are you a Roman Catholic?", that person could reply in the very strictest sense of the term: "Yes, I am a Roman Catholic. I belong to the local Church of Rome. The Bishop of my local Church is Benedict XVI."

Now, lest you misunderstand the point I am trying to make, let me hasten to ask another question: "Is there a true sense in which you and I, who are Rochester Catholics can also be said to be Roman Catholics?" The answer of course is: Yes. We are not, it should be clear, Roman Catholics in the same sense that Catholics living in Rome are Roman Catholics. We are Roman Catholics in another, but important sense. We are Roman Catholics, because the local Church of Rochester is united with the local Church of Rome in a unique way. What do I mean? Simply this: throughout the world there exists a fellowship (or sisterhood, if you prefer) of local churches, to which the local Church of Rochester is joined. This fellowship of churches would include the Church of Chicago, New York, Paris, Montreal, Youngstown (Ohio), Rome, etc. What is it that unites these various churches so that they constitute a true fellowship? It is, among other things, the very important fact that one of these local churches is the center and visible sign of the unity of the Churches. And the Church which is at the center of Catholic unity is the local Church of Rome. The head of the local church of Rome -- because this church is at the center -- is called the Pope, a name which means "Father."

The heads of the other local churches throughout the world have authority in their local churches, not as delegates of the Pope, but rather have an authority that comes from God. Vatican II asserted that the bishops of local churches are vicars of Christ. They are not office managers for the bishop of Rome. Together with the Pope and with him as their leader, they constitute what we call the College of Bishops. It is this College, under the headship of the Pope, that has supreme authority in the Church.

So, each local Bishop has from God the authority to govern and serve his own local church. Together in union with the Pope and not apart from him, they share in a concern for the whole church. That is why the Second Vatican Council was so important an event in the life of the contemporary Church. For it brought together in one place all the Bishops with the Pope as their head.

So, we are Roman Catholics, because of our link with other local churches that find their center in the local church of Rome. But -- what I want to stress -- is that it is in the local church of Rochester that we experience the reality of Church. It is in the local Church that we become conscious of ourselves as "Easter People." For it is in the local church that we are initiated, by baptism, confirmation and first Eucharist, into the People of God who are the Body of Christ. It is in the local church that the Gospel is proclaimed for us and by us. It is in the local church that we gather as the family of God, to celebrate the Eucharistic Meal, in which we experience our communion with one another in the Lord Jesus and our ever-growing awareness of God's Presence in our lives.

It is in the context of the local church that we experience the joys and sorrows, the agonies and ecstasies, the certainties and the perplexities that go along with being Christian People on pilgrimage toward the full consummation of what it means to be "Easter People": that final handing over to God when God shall be All in All. It is in the local church that we talk about the things that we believe and strive to live the Gospel values to which we have committed ourselves.

In the local Church, the Bishop is the leader. But for his leadership to work, he needs to be in contact with the people of the local Church. There must be dialogue in the local Church. That is why we, the local Church of Rochester, some years ago completed a Synod in which all the people of the local Church came together to discuss what the priorities of the Church ought to be at the present time.

What I am saying is that what has happened to the Church in the wake of Vatican II is that we have come to realize that in its essence the Church is more egalitarian than hierarchical. By this I mean that baptism is more important than orders. Hence, when I think of Church, I think, first of all of the fact that all the members of the

Church are equal, because all have been baptized into Christ

     Some are chosen from out of that equality to serve the rest of the members in various ways. This what we mean by the sacrament of Orders. Ordination is a call from God to some of the baptized to serve all the baptized. Those who are called to the performance of certain functions in the Church on behalf of the whole Church, are not higher or better than the rest of the baptized. Rather they are servants of their sisters and brothers. And if they are to minister well they must be in dialogue with the whole community of the Church.

2. Clarifying Our Understanding of the Role of the Bishops

In the wake of Vatican II we have come to realize that in its essence the church is more egalitarian that hierarchical. By this I mean that baptism is more important than orders. Hence, when I think of church, I think first of all that all of the members of the church are equal because all are baptized into Christ.

Some are chosen from that equality to serve the rest of the members in various ways. This is what we mean by the sacrament of orders. Ordination is a call from God to some of the baptized to serve all of the baptized. Those who are called to the performance of certain functions in the church on behalf of the whole church are not higher or better than the rest of the baptized. Rather they are servants of their sisters and brothers. And if they are to minister well they must be in dialogue with the whole community of the church.

Vatican II asserted that the bishops of local churches are vicars of Christ. They are not office managers for the Bishop of Rome. Together with the Pope and with him as their leader, they constitute what we call the College of Bishops. It is this college, under the headship of the pope that has supreme authority in the church. The council made clear that the bishops of the church are the successors of the apostles. Each bishop exercises authority over his own diocese. The bishops as a body exercise complete authority over the church. In the course of time as we shall see one bishop, the Bishop of Rome rose to a position of prominence.

When we speak of the pope we must remember that the papacy is not a higher order that would put a person one step above bishops. No, the Pope is simply a bishop. He is the Bishop of Rome, just as Timothy Dolan is Bishop of New York. It is true that the Bishop of Rome has always occupied a special place in the church. In the early church the word pope was used sometimes for bishops, sometimes even for priests. It was not until the time of the Gregorian Reform at the beginning of the Second Millennium that the title pope was claimed solely for the Bishop of Rome. The pope began to exercise authority that would not have been understood by the bishops of Rome in the First Millennium. It was also at this time that time the bishop of Rome claimed to the title of Vicar of Christ and not simply the Vicar of Peter as the Pope had always heretofore been called. (Incidentally I want to say that Vatican II said that all bishops are Vicars of Christ.)

A Look At History

Many Catholics believe that the papacy has always exercised the authority it presently does. Many still believe that the pope is the head of the church and that the bishops are really office managers acting in his name. A quick look at history belies such a view. It shows just how much the papacy has changed over the centuries. The Petrine ministry as it is exercised today, at the beginning of the third millennium, would hardly have been recognized by the popes and bishops of the first millennium. Let me offer a simple example of what I mean.

The First Millenium

During the first millennium the Bishop of Rome, since Rome was the city in which Peter and Paul had been martyred, exercised a leadership role in the Church. Bishops of other churches often looked to the Bishop of Rome for help in resolving doctrinal and disciplinary matters. Further, the Bishop of Rome did not hesitate to speak out, when the unity of the church seemed to be threatened. But, all this being said, the history is still clear: no bishop of Rome ever claimed the right to exercise authority over the other churches, much less to appoint their bishops. He saw himself as a bishop among bishops, with the special role of serving the unity of the universal church, protecting the integrity of the Gospel and at times acting as spokesperson for his brother bishops. The bishops were united collegially with one another or, to quote the words of Pope John Paul II: they were "linked in a union of faith and sacramental life."

During the first millennium the bishop of Rome was chosen by the clergy and laity of Rome. *Up until the ninth century the Roman Church never chose as its bishop someone who was already a bishop elsewhere.* Hence the election in 882 of Marinus I to succeed Pope John VIII as bishop of Rome was a significant departure from this long-standing tradition. While Marinus had served in the church of Rome as archdeacon to Pope John VIII, he was --when elected to the Roman see -- already the bishop of Caere in Tuscany. This means, as the *Oxford Dictionary of Popes* says that "he was the first bishop of another see to be elected pope." It was a precedent-setting event that would have far-reaching effects in the second millennium.

I believe that Pope Gregory the Great (the bishop of Rome who died in 609) expressed well the attitude that modem day Rome might well emulate. Writing to Patriarch Eulogius of Alexandria, he says: "Your Beatitude speaks to me saying 'as you have commanded,'". Gregory chides Eulogius for such a manner of speaking; "I must ask you, not to use such words in speaking of me, for I know what I am and what you are. In rank you are my brothers, in manner of life my fathers."

He goes on to say: "Therefore I have not given orders, but have simply done my best to indicate what I think useful." How much more helpful it would have been to the church and how much loyalty to church leadership would have been generated, if the Vatican, when addressing, say, the issue of the ordination of women, had said: "I am not giving orders, but simply doing my best to indicate what I think useful."

Such an approach would be an admirable way of generating some harmony between a Matthean ecclesiology and a Johannine one. To create such harmony between theological positions, which so easily can be at cross purposes with one another, is surely one of the great challenges the church faces in the third millennium.

Yet the challenge must be faced, if today's church is to be faithful to the insight of the early Church, the Church Catholic, which chose to receive into its canon of inspired scripture, not just Matthew but also John, not just John but also Matthew. It must be ready to continue to live with the inevitable tensions which that choice has necessarily bequeathed to the church.

The Second Millenium

The eleventh century witnessed drastic changes in the understanding of the Petrine ministry. Pope Gregory VII (1073-1085) introduced what has been called the Gregorian Reform. During the eleventh century unworthy persons were appointed as bishops. Pope Gregory made drastic changes in the church. This so called Gregorian Reform, among other things reserved the title "pope" exclusively to the bishop of Rome. Pope Gregory VII a man of exceptional talent, made reform the keystone of his pontificate, at a time when reform was desperately needed in the church. He had an exalted mystique of the papacy, describing himself as "universal pastor" and claiming the right to appoint and depose bishops. He even claimed authority in the secular order and the right to depose emperors and kings.

A century later, Innocent III (1198-1216), with an equally exalted concept of his office, saw the pope as above the church rather than in the Church, "set midway between God and man, below God, but above men, given not only the universal church but the whole world to govern." A huge job description, though hardly a modest one! He changed the designation of his office from what it had been up to his time ("Vicar of Peter") to the more exalted title of "Vicar of Christ." He said of himself: "Although successor of the prince of the apostles, we are not his vicar or that of any man or apostle; we are vicars of Christ himself." It comes as no surprise that one of the decrees of the Fourth Lateran Council (1215), which he convoked, stated: "The Roman Church through the Lord's disposition has a primacy of ordinary power over all other churches inasmuch as it is the mother and mistress of all Christ's faithful."

During the next few centuries the powers of the bishop of Rome waxed and waned, as the papacy became more and more involved in the politics of the Empire and the developing European nation states. In the nineteenth century the First Vatican Council (1869-70) established the "blueprint" for the understanding of the papal office that would dominate Roman Catholic thought till the Second Vatican Council. Vatican I defined the primacy and infallibility of the bishop of Rome.

Vatican I

Vatican I was a summing up of the understanding of the papacy that had been developing during the second millennium. Its dogmatic Constitution on the Church, *Pastor aeternus*, is a reprise of the teaching of Gregory VII and Innocent III:

We teach and declare that, by divine ordinance, the Roman church possesses a preeminence of ordinary power over every other church and that this jurisdictional power of the Roman Pontiff is both episcopal and immediate. Both clergy and faithful ...are bound to submit to this power...and this not only in matters concerning faith and morals, but also those which regard the discipline and government of the church throughout the world.

The document attempts to respond to a question that the above statement must surely bring to mind, namely, what effect does so strong an assertion of papal power have on the authority of bishops of local churches? The answer is ambiguous at best: "The power of the supreme pontiff by no means detracts from the ordinary and immediate power of episcopal jurisdiction. For the bishops are successors of the apostles and by appointment of the Holy Spirit to govern the particular flock entrusted to them."

In all fairness it must be said that the Council did not have the time to discuss in detail the authority of bishops, as with the outbreak of the Franco-Prussian war, the Council was adjourned for an indefinite time. It was never reconvened.

In one very significant area, Vatican I was more than a reprise of previous second millennium thinking. For in that same document, *Pastor aeternus,* it defined a doctrine that had given rise to much discussion both outside the Roman Catholic Church and within: infallibility. The Council said that, when the Roman Pontiff defines a truth *ex cathedra*, he possesses the divine assistance promised to blessed Peter, namely, that infallibility which the divine Redeemer willed his church to enjoy in defining doctrine concerning faith or morals."

Vatican II

Vatican II, in its constitution on the church, attempted to establish a balance between the power of the pope and that of the bishops. This was an important step, since, in the years following Vatican I, a mentality (untrue to that Council's teaching) became widespread in the church, namely, the belief that the pope ran the church and the bishops were simply his delegates, acting in his stead among all the faithful. Vatican II changed this mentality. It asserts very clearly that the bishops govern the churches over which they preside and do so as vicars of Christ. "The power which they exercise personally in the name of Christ is proper, ordinary and immediate." It makes clear that "they are not to be considered as vicars of the Roman Pontiffs, because they exercise a power that is proper to them." Vatican II recovered that sense of collegiality among the bishops of the church in union with the bishop of Rome that characterized the church of the first millennium.

It may be said that Vatican II supplemented Vatican I, though it did not replace it. Like Vatican I it asserted the primacy and infallibility of the pope, but in a context of collegiality. The pope is the subject of infallibility, but so are the bishops of the universal church in union with the pope their head. Ideally the pope speaks in union with all the bishops, but even in certain circumstances, when he speaks alone, he speaks as head of the college of bishops.

Do We Really Need The Pope?

I recall a conversation that I had with a dear friend of mine in England: the late Canon A.M. Allchin an Anglican priest and highly regarded theologian. I put the question to him: "Do we need the pope?" His answer was immediate and unequivocal. "Yes indeed," he said, "the papacy is an indispensable element of the Church." "Why do you say that?" I asked. His answer: "The Christian church is a historical religion. And the role of the bishop of Rome is unquestionably an essential part of that history." He spoke of the meeting some years ago at Assisi, to which Pope John Paul II invited people representing various religions. At the time my friend was canon residentiary at Canterbury Cathedral. He recalled a remark of Robert Runcie, the archbishop of Canterbury who had attended the

Assisi meeting: "Only the pope could have called such a meeting."

As I have already made clear the papacy has changed in substantive ways over the centuries. My English friend whom I referred to above would say, as would many other Christians, that one of the crucial issues calling for ecumenical dialogue today is this: *is it possible to rethink the primacy of the pope, as it is presently exercised, in the light of what it was in the first millennium?* This is no easy task. The issue is: can this be done in a creative way: that is, not simply by a return to the papacy of the first millennium, but by a sincere effort to allow what the papal ministry was then *to enable us to see, in ways not yet fully discernible, what the papal ministry can become today?*

Recent Papal Actions

Recent actions on the part of the papacy have made it difficult for us to see how its present mode of acting is in any way similar to the way the bishop of Rome operated in the first millennium. We have to find the church in which the Holy Spirit is operative. Will this be found in the hierarchy or must we look elsewhere today? Some years ago in 1964, Thomas Merton wrote: "I personally think that we are paralyzed by institutionalizism, formalization, rigidity, and regression." The real life of the church he says, "is not in her hierarchy, it is dormant somewhere."

Elsewhere in 1967, Merton wrote to Dorothy Day: "The moral insensitivity of those in authority on certain points so utterly crucial for the church has to be pointed out and if possible dispelled." He goes on to say later in this letter, "what is a church after all but a community in which truth is shared, not a monopoly that dispenses it from the top down. Light travels on a two way street in our church; or I hope it does."

In recent years we have seen more than enough instances of insensitivity on the part of the hierarchy. We have seen bishops invited to resign because they called for a discussion on the issue of the ordination of women. The Vatican refuses to allow even a discussion of that issue and this is simply unintelligible.

Further, the English speaking church is faced with the task of introducing a new Missal for use in the Catholic Church. This is despite the fact that in 1998, a new translation of the Missal had been approved by all the English speaking bishops. The Vatican decided to act against the will of the English speaking bishops and produce a new version of the Missal that many people believed is inferior to the ICEL version of 1998. The power of bishops to regulate matters for their local churches was simply suspended. Unfortunately the bishops were not strong enough to say no to the Vatican and insist on having its own translation.

Father Anthony Ruff, O.S.B., a Benedictine monk of St. John's Abbey, and a professor of liturgy who was on the ICEL Commission has said, "The forth coming missal is but a part of a larger pattern of top-down impositions by a central authority that does not think itself accountable to the larger church. When I think of how secretive the translation process was, how little consultation was done with priests or laity... how unsatisfactory the final text is, how this text was imposed on National Conferences of Bishops in violation of their legitimate Episcopal authority, how much deception and mischief have marked this process- and then when I think of our Lord's teachings on service and love and unity...I weep." (*America,* February 14, 2011)

The sense of collegiality that was so important a part of Vatican II seems to be rapidly disappearing. The Second Vatican Council asserted that bishops were the Vicars of Christ in their own local churches. But it appears that their authority to act in their own dioceses is gradually being eroded by decisions made at the top. It seems today that the pope is not just the ultimate authority in the church; but the only authority. John O'Malley, the dean of American Catholic Historians in an article written in 2001, described what is happening in the Catholic Church as the papalization of Roman Catholicism (*America,* 2001).

And Yet...

In a meeting on September 25, 2011 as he was ending his visit to Germany, Pope Benedict XVI pointed out that, "For some decades now we have been experiencing a decline in religious practice and we have been seeing substantial numbers of the baptized drifting away from church life. This prompts the question; should the church not change?"

"The church", he explained, "is not just other people, not just the hierarchy, the pope and the bishops; we are all church, we the baptized... yes, there are grounds for change. There is need for change. Every Christian in the community of the faithful is constantly called to change...As far as the church is concerned, though the basic motive for change is the apostolic mission of the disciples and the church herself.

The church in other words must constantly rededicate herself to her mission, he added, explaining that this mission embraces three aspects; bearing witness, making disciples in all nations and proclaiming the gospel.

Does this seem to sound like the call for change that is in the introduction to this book? Does this sound similar to what Newman said about the necessity of change???

A Quotation

How baffling you are, oh Church, and yet how I love you!

How you have made me suffer and yet how much I owe you!

I would like to see you destroyed, and yet I need your presence.

You have given me so much scandal, and yet you have made me understand what sanctity is.

I have seen nothing in the world more devoted to obscurity, more compromised, more false,

And yet I have touched nothing more pure, more generous, more beautiful.

How often I have wanted to shut the doors of my soul in your face.

And how often I have prayed to die in the safety of your arms.

No I cannot free myself from you because I am you, though not completely

And besides, where would I go? Would I establish another church?

I would not be able to establish it without the same faults for they are the same faults I carry in me.

And if I did establish another, it would be my Church, not the Church of Christ.

I am old enough to know that I am no better than anyone else.

--Carlo Carretto

EPILOGUE

Joy and Hope!

The Second Vatican Council concluded its deliberations on a note of joy and hope, embodied in the document on the Church in the Modern World (*Gaudium et Spes*).

I want to bring my book to a conclusion by referring once again to this document.

It was a completely revolutionary document in the history of the church. For some 1500 years the church lived in the shadow of St. Augustine's book, *The City of God*. One of the great classics of western literature --that probably few people read today -- it is a huge book, both in length and in the breadth of its vision. He wrote it in the beginning of the fifth century when civilization as he knew it seemed about to collapse. He describes two cities: the city of God and the earthly city. "These two cities," Augustine writes, "were made by two loves: the earthly city by the love of self unto the contempt of God, the heavenly city by the love of God unto the contempt of self." (Bk. 4, c. 28) Under the influence of this perspective the church thought of itself as committed to the growth of the City of God and the departure of the City of Man. Eschatology, it would seem has trumped incarnational thinking.

The Second Vatican Council, while surely committed to the City of God, turned to the City of Man and the problems and concerns that are there. *Gaudium et Spes* begins with these words, "The joys and the hopes, the griefs, and the anxieties, of men and women of this age, especially those who are poor or in any way afflicted, these too are the joys and hopes, the grief's and anxieties of the followers of Christ. Indeed nothing genuinely human fails to raise an echo in their hearts." (GS.1) This is clearly incarnational thinking. Article 22 makes this even clearer; "By His incarnation the Son of God has united Himself in some fashion with every human being. He worked with human hands. He thought with a human mind, acted by human choice and loved with a human heart. Born of the Virgin Mary, He has truly been made one of us, like us in all things except sin."

    This commitment of the church to the joys and sorrows of the world in which we live is, in my opinion, the new direction that the church will take in the Third Millennium. All this takes place in a context in which members of the church who by and large have become educated and capable of thinking for themselves. This is why we find the people of God more and more clamoring to speak out in their church. More and more they believe they have a right to a voice in the life and direction of the church.

    The church of the First Millennium was the church of the bishops. The church of the Second Millennium was the church of the popes. May we hope that the Third Millennium is becoming the church of the people of God.

****

This is my hope for the church of today and tomorrow.

Gaudium et Spes   Joy and Hope!